CLAIRE I

Claire Eastham is a Manchester-based author, award-winning mental health blogger, campaigner and keynote speaker. Regarded as one of the UK's foremost mental health bloggers, Claire's witty and self-deprecating sense of humour has seen her attract thousands of readers to her blog, *We're All Mad Here*. Claire's first book of the same name sold out its entire first print run in just five days and was selected for Reading Well Books on Prescription in 2018.

Claire is an ambassador for the mental health research charity, MQ, and has regularly appeared on TV and radio, including appearances on *This Morning*, *BBC Breakfast*, and across BBC Radio.

CLAIRE EASTHAM

How I Learned to Live with Panic

VINTAGE

13 5 7 9 10 8 6 4 2

Vintage is part of the Penguin Random House group of companies whose addresses can be found at global.penguinrandomhouse.com

Penguin
Random House
UK

Copyright © Claire Eastham 2021

Claire Eastham has asserted her right to be identified as the author of this Work in accordance with the Copyright, Designs and Patents Act 1988

First published in Vintage in 2022
First published under the title *F**k, I Think I'm Dying*
in trade paperback by Square Peg in 2021

penguin.co.uk/vintage

A CIP catalogue record for this book is available from the British Library

ISBN 9781529112603

Printed and bound in Great Britain by Clays Ltd, Elcograf S.p.A.

The authorised representative in the EEA is Penguin Random House Ireland, Morrison Chambers, 32 Nassau Street, Dublin D02 YH68

Penguin Random House is committed to a sustainable future for our business, our readers and our planet. This book is made from Forest Stewardship Council® certified paper.

Contents

Preface: The New Normal

This book was originally scheduled for publication in October 2020 ... but then the world went up in flames and plans were altered.

On 23 March 2020, the UK went into lockdown for the first time, something that feels like a lifetime ago to me now. Like everyone else, I watched Boris Johnson address the nation (you know you're fucked when it's a 'special announcement' from the BBC). He told us; "*from this evening I must give the British people a very simple instruction – you must stay at home*", and that was that. (Although we later found out that there were indeed a few loopholes for Tory MPs.)

It's not that I didn't really take it in beforehand – the seriousness of the pandemic, I mean. I had, after all, heard the stats and read about the strain on hospitals, the plight of care homes and lack of available medical assistance. I'd witnessed the queues outside of the supermarkets, the panic to buy milk and bog roll. (I said I wouldn't, then caved and bought a pack of twenty-four!) I knew that my parents were stuck in Germany and my brother in Canada, and that I had two elderly grandparents who I needed to make sure had food (one, who you'll meet in chapter seven, only accepted the seriousness of the situation when the bingo closed).

On one of our daily fifteen-minute walks 'for exercise', my husband and I passed number 36 on our street and saw grandchildren holding up drawings to the window, chatting animatedly to their grandparents inside. As the weeks went on the yearning and confusion became a wound to children everywhere, who didn't understand why they couldn't embrace 'Nana' or 'Grandad'. Alas, these were not the things that shocked me; they were drip-fed slowly over time, as the world imploded.

What did shock me, however, was the rapid – and in some cases dramatic – decline in the mental health of people I knew and cared for. As a veteran of panic and anxiety, I'm aware of the early signs, the symptoms (both mental and physical) and how to manage them. For the first time, I experienced panic and anxiety as an observer. I saw it in the eyes of the people I loved, heard it in their voices and observed it in their bodies. 'What's happening to me?' One friend cried, 'something's wrong, but I don't know what.'

From experience, I understand that confusion can be just as powerful as fear. Not understanding what is happening to you is a very frightening thing indeed. (Also, I'd be lying if I said I didn't use the opportunity to point out; 'see, I told you panic was fucking terrifying!') I realised how ill-equipped people were at dealing with mental anguish when it struck. I don't mean this as a criticism, as it made sense on a fundamental level. Mental wellbeing was not prioritised by people of my generation and older. This cemented my belief that mental health education should be paramount in the workplace and not merely dependent on those lunchtime 'mental wellbeing presentations' organised by HR maybe once a year ... and let's be honest, 50 per cent of us go for the free lunch!

During the first lockdown I received maybe fifty direct messages on both Instagram and Twitter, from people asking for advice. By the end of the second lockdown, it was 400. Kindness became the greatest, and in many cases only, available therapy.

I hoped then and continue to hope that this book will provide comfort for those experiencing panic; that it will ground the reader in the realisation that although overwhelming, panic attacks can be both understood and managed.

The COVID-19 pandemic has battered all of us over the course of two years, whether in large, violent ways, or death by a thousand papercuts. Approaching 2022, I'm hopeful that we can gradually begin to heal, or at the very least have a two-week holiday in the sun!

Introduction

Allow me to be frank from the first sentence.

My name is Claire Eastham and I have, to date, **experienced 371 panic attacks over a seven-year period. An average of fifty-three per year.** I live with panic. **Panic is in my veins and we cohabit; we're roommates, lovers, enemies and all the rest.** There are times when I notice it more, poking me, taunting me, knocking me off course, and times when I barely register its existence at all.

I understand the psychology of a panic attack, the purpose of one, the symptoms (physical, mental and emotional), the drugs used to sedate them and the therapy devised to find the root causes. I know it all, truly. I've been writing about mental health for nearly a decade, translating medical jargon and making coping techniques more accessible. I have an award-winning blog, I'm an ambassador for a national charity, and my first book *We're All Mad Here* sold out its entire first print run in just four days. This, along with personal experience and obsessive research, makes me an expert. Self-made, I might add. I can't follow up this claim with a medical qualification, but I'm an expert all the same.

There is no cure for panic attacks. No magic wand I can wave, or snake oil I could flog. This is *not* a self-help book. A self-help book implies that a cure lies hidden somewhere within the contents. I have no method to share or solution to sell. But don't lose heart just yet, because what I do have to impart is experience, and I pledge that with a little work and understanding, panic attacks do not have to control you. They won't stop you from working, socialising or living a fulfilling life. We can remove their power.

There might not be an officially recognised cure, but what we can do is learn how to communicate with panic. We can learn what triggers our attacks, how to stop the attacks from being triggered in error and how to deal with them when they are triggered.

I learned how to communicate with panic the long and hard way, through a variety of experiences and complete fuck-ups. Not that I'd change anything. Fuck-ups are how I've learned the majority of life's lessons. I'm not saying this as an affirmation, or even to be used as inspiration. It's a fact: mistakes make for a superior teacher.

Before we start, I feel I should warn you that I am what some people may find to be a frustrating person. I've made the same mistakes repeatedly in my life, particularly when it comes to mental health, to the point of pure idiocy. My anger is short-lived but explosive, I'm emotional, chronically insecure, opinionated and a bit of a gobshite after a few drinks. I overthink things to the point of self-indulgence, care too much what people think, hurt too easily, and I swear A LOT. Positivity doesn't come naturally to me, whereas, cynicism is part of my DNA. I make jokes when I'm uncomfortable and I struggle with affirmations such as: 'It's OK *not* to be OK,' or 'You're not alone,' because honestly, I don't find them at all fucking useful when I'm the one rolling around on the bathroom floor.

Still, I'm also funny, generous, kind, ridiculous, perceptive, reasonably smart, loyal, honest and my bark is worse than any bite I could deliver.

If you trust nothing else, then trust that I AM a panic attack expert. Panic is something I live with, like IBS or eczema. It's not ideal, but we make it work. Even during the darkest periods, panic has NEVER controlled my life and I can help anyone who reads this to change their attitude towards panic attacks. That's a promise.

All the rest is just white noise and jesting.

CHAPTER 1

To Hell and Back: Learning to Let People Help You and the True Art of Self-care

> Trigger warning: This chapter contains graphic descriptions of panic attacks and deals with the topic of self-harm.

Friday 29th September 2019, 12.48 a.m.

My head jerks back violently and collides with the concrete wall. I don't register the impact, it barely signifies. My jaw clicks loudly and my mouth sags. I vomit again from the pain, as my neck spasms. I've spent seven hours, seven fucking hours in hell, without a single moment of respite. I twitch and pulse, tremble and convulse ... and the pain is so overwhelming I see stars. I'm sweating, my mouth is like sandpaper and I'm frightened, terrified in fact.

Dan, my husband, will later comment that I looked possessed, as though a demon was trying to claw its way out of my face.

Panic attacks are nothing new to me. I've been experiencing them sporadically for years and have already survived one mental breakdown. I've built a solid reputation as an authority in mental health over a three-year period. I preach about treating the brain with the same respect as the body and looking out for the 'warning signs'. So, with all of my valuable knowledge and experience, what am I doing here? How have I found myself face down on a kota stone floor, wishing I was dead?

Forty-eight hours prior to this, I was on the M5, travelling back from Cheltenham. I'd taken part in a panel event with other mental health experts and hated every moment of it. I was exhausted and uncomfortable, but spent the evening pretending to be fine. The irony being that while on stage talking about panic, I was experiencing back-to-back attacks.

I completed the seven-hour round trip in one evening, rather than staying overnight at the hotel with the other speakers, as would have been the sensible decision. Due to road closures I didn't get home until around 1 a.m., then stayed up until 3 trying to wind down and was up again at 7 for a business trip to London.

It had been an incredibly busy period. On top of my normal work duties, I'd secured a second book deal and was working non-stop to a deadline that may have been achievable if I hadn't then seen the house of my dreams and moved in a month away from the first draft deadline. We had contractors and decorators in for weeks, making the environment chaotic, then to make matters worse, I contracted flu just as Dan was away with work.

The first red flag occurred the day before Cheltenham. Along with a huge panic attack, I developed a headache that quickly became a migraine. I wasn't concerned though, as I occasionally got migraines when my period was due. Yet my period didn't arrive. Was I pregnant? The £1.50 test from Tesco said no. I took painkillers and waited for it to pass. It didn't. I went to sleep in pain, felt pain in my dreams and woke up to pain. My head throbbed constantly. It made me flinch, slouch and eventually vomit. By the time I woke up on Thursday morning for London, the sight in my left eye was blurry, as though I'd been drinking for several hours. *This isn't OK. You know it isn't.*

I considered ringing my friend and cancelling my appearance at her event that evening. Deep down I knew she would understand, but then, lots of people from the mental health community would be there and I convinced myself that this was an opportunity I shouldn't miss. *You can have a lie-in and rest tomorrow.*

Maybe it wasn't about supporting my friend at all, maybe I had selfish reasons. Was I afraid of being forgotten within the mental health world? The media and personal insecurities have a way of stoking that fire. Making us (or me) behave recklessly. Or maybe I was in complete denial by this point, and simply too afraid to stop.

The Uber driver who took me to Manchester Piccadilly noticed the tension. 'You don't look very well,' he said softly. Taxi drivers have heard some of my darkest, or most ridiculous thoughts over the years. Their kind curiosity, mixed with the knowledge that I'll probably never see them again, makes me sing like a canary: *I'm worried that I'm infertile; Sometimes I think I'll be dead by the age of forty. I think I'm going to give up this writing shit and start a walking service for shy dogs.*

So, I used the opportunity to tell Usman the truth. 'I'm travelling to London on only two hours' sleep,' I blurt out, 'and I live with an acute mental health disorder. I'm exhausted and my head hurts so much I think I might collapse, but I promised my friend that I'd be at her event tonight. I've cancelled on her previously and I don't want to get a reputation for being flaky. The plan is just to get through today. Then everything will be OK.'

The look on his face tells me what I already know myself, deep down: I shouldn't be here. I should be at home resting, not sitting in his car.

By now the vision in my left eye has all but vanished, there are only shadows. *You can't fucking see. Do you understand? You're blind in one eye. This isn't OK.* I cover the right one, deliberately trying to jump-start the left. But it remains in darkness. I get on the train, because I don't know what else to do. When you live in the land of denial for so long, it can be hard to leave.

I do, however, send this message to my three best friends:

Can someone check in with me in a few hours? I feel unhinged ... like something isn't right. Haven't felt like this is in a long time. Maybe it's hormones messing with my head? (I'd recently come off the Pill.) *I don't know. I don't feel safe.*

Once in London, I meet my friend Natasha at a pub near the venue and it's on the tip of my tongue to tell her the truth: 'Tash, I think I'm in trouble. I don't feel safe. I need you to help me get home.' But I don't say a word, I ask about her kitten and we laugh over white wine for an hour. It's nice, a welcome distraction after being stuck in my head for hours. I feel hopeful: maybe everything will calm down after all?

I don't remember much of the night after that, nor the train journey back to Manchester. Not because of the wine. I stopped drinking when I arrived at the event, afraid that dehydration would only increase the pain. What I do recall, however, is wedging my head between the seats in front of me, like a vice. The pressure provided some relief from the throbbing. I didn't care how bizarre I looked, and at some point, I must've blacked out.

The following morning, I went to see a doctor who prescribed me Paramax (basically paracetamol mixed with a nausea suppressant). By this point, my eyesight had returned, but the pain and nausea were still intense.

8

I felt the first twinge in my jaw that evening around 7 p.m. I was watching TV at the time, as Dan tucked into a curry. I tried to ignore the sensation. After all, I got aches all the time, and presumed it would just sort itself out, as my left eye had. Unfortunately, the ache in question rapidly turned into a throb and after twenty minutes, a spasm of pure agony. Imagine the worst cramp you've ever experienced. Now imagine that cramp in your sodding jaw.

You've finally done it, you've killed yourself. Panic latched on to the pain like a dog with a bone. I was struggling to breathe and my heart pounded so hard it made my chest ache. I was sweating and trembling, desperately trying to steady myself. Is this a panic attack? Or is this the real deal? In six years, I'd never experienced a symptom like this, my entire face was vibrating. A part of me hoped I'd had an allergic reaction to the Paramax, that could at least be treated.

I ran around the house in agony, up and down the stairs, I went into the garden barefoot, I had a cold shower, put ice on my jaw – anything that might ease the pain.

Eventually, at midnight, as I lay vomiting and convulsing on the bedroom floor, Dan called for an ambulance.

The paramedics arrive, and I immediately apologise for wasting their time, before blurting out: 'Please don't let me die!' What a shitshow for them. A grown woman rolling around on the floor, in just a T-shirt and big faded knickers, begging theatrically for her life. Both of the women are kind, unexpectedly so, but one of them in particular, Lorraine, is incredible. I don't know what I was expecting, but I didn't expect her. She holds my hand, tries to make me laugh, doesn't judge and engages me in conversation. I know what she's trying to do, even though I wish I didn't. A curse of being an expert in mental health is that you're acquainted with every trick in the book. Her 'distraction' techniques aren't going to work on my fucker of a brain.

At one point she holds my jaw in her hands to feel the spasming herself. She then grabs a pillow off the bed, places it on the floor and suggests a yoga position that might help. Unfortunately, before I can move into place, my dog Rigby sees her chance for additional comfort and collapses on to the pillow with a thud, pleased with her decision!

After observing me for a while longer, Lorraine squeezes my hand firmly and says, 'You're not well at all are you, sweetheart? I can see that. I'm going to take you to hospital, and we'll get you some help.'

I burst into tears, realising only then that I'd been waiting for someone to give me permission to fall apart, to be afraid and to ask for help. She grants me all of the above and whisks me away on her great white horse, aptly disguised as an ambulance. However, before we depart, she does recommend that I put on some trousers.

Dan takes Rigby to my mum's house and tells me he'll meet me at the hospital. Lorraine stays with me until I'm fully checked in, and I notice her failure to reveal the history of my mental health, initially at least. When she does utter the words 'anxiety' and 'panic attacks' I see the interest on the nurse's face shift, and I know that I've been automatically dropped to the bottom of the list. 'She's been living with it for several years and manages it very well by herself. This pain isn't normal for her and she isn't coping with it. I think she's experiencing nervous exhaustion.' (A polite way of saying a breakdown.) I listen to Lorraine pleading my case and I love her for it, but we both know I'm fucked. When she has to leave, I give her a big hug and thank her for her kindness.

After my bloods are taken, I'm directed to another public waiting room, in which a young twenty-something boy with blue hair is sitting across from me. He's drinking from a large can of Monster and talking into his phone, 'Nah, they don't know shit, mate! Apparently, I just collapsed at the bar. Yeah, it's bad, I'm in A&E now, having some tests done and that. My manager thought I was dead!' He then proceeds to call several people in his contacts, repeating the story and laughing, full of bravado. When fifteen minutes later a woman who I presume to be his mum turns up, he sobs like a child and she feeds him a Mars bar. I'd quite like my mum and a Mars bar right about now too.

I rock back and forth in my seat, trying to drop anchor and stabilise. *It's just panic. It's a really bad panic attack*, I chant internally. A sharp cramp slams into the left side of my jaw, momentarily blurring my vision. Am I going to pass out? I hope so. I feel the urge to vomit rise up and dart towards the nearest loo. Blood and bile are projected into the toilet bowl and I soothe my burning throat by gargling water. I catch sight of my reflection in the mirror and I'm shocked by what I see. My eyes are bloodshot, some vessels have burst, making me look like a zombie, I'm deathly pale and my jaw won't stop twitching. Did I swallow a parasite in London and just not realise? As I'm washing my hands, drops of blood appear, littering the basin and mixing with the swirling water like tie-dye. It's my nose. I don't need the mirror to confirm this; the metallic taste in my mouth is evident.

'Please,' I say to the nurse. 'I know that I'm no more important than anyone else here, but I'm in agony. I don't know how much longer I can handle it.' By now I sound as though my tongue has swollen to three times its natural size, making my speech unnatural. 'Is there anything you can do to help?'

She looks at me briefly and replies: 'Nobody jumps the queue, perhaps you should try some fresh air?'

A key point to highlight here: an overworked nurse in A&E is unlikely to pick up on the signs of a panic attack, so despite her frosty demeanour I wasn't offended and I'm still not. It was a Friday night and I expect she thought I was drunk.

Pain has a way of separating a person from both their vanity and rational thought. You only have to talk to a woman who's experienced childbirth to understand that. I would've done anything for gas and air at that point, anything for even a five-second respite. *I'll run into a wall, strip naked, smash a vase over my head, ANYTHING.* I burst into fits of giggles that I try to suppress.

The idea comes to me like a bolt of lightning. *There's a motorway literally outside the main hospital entrance.* I feel a buzz of excitement. *If I get hit by a car, then they'll have to help. It'll force their hand. Best-case scenario, I'll lose consciousness and wake up in a bed on a ward.* I have no intention of dying and my biggest concern is for the welfare of the driver of my accident car. I would need to plan this. I reason that if a car clocked under 30mph then I can jump, hit the bonnet sideways and be thrown forwards without receiving a life-threatening injury. Maybe a few broken bones, or a laceration to the shoulder. The driver would hopefully be unharmed, and the vehicle suffer only superficial damage.

The pain in my jaw is now so entwined with panic that I've reached a state of mania. *Do it! You need to do this, or you'll explode.*

What other options do you have? Your jaw is about to split. There's no other way out.

I rise decisively from the chair, walk down the corridor and through the maze that is Salford Royal hospital. I just have to get outside, clear my head and then I can choose a spot. I'm not afraid; I'm a woman with a goal. The pain alters my vision somewhat as I stagger forward and I begin to see double. *Just keep going. You can do this. Don't be sick here, they might stop you.*

However, as I round the final corner triumphantly, I come face to face with Dan, who's just arrived.

'What are you doing?' he asks.

'I'm going to throw myself in front of a car.' I reply matter-of-factly, sure of my plan. 'It's totally fine, babe, I've thought about it, and this is my best option.'

He doesn't react but puts his arm firmly around my shoulders and guides me to the car park instead for some 'fresh air'. My plans have been scuppered.

After that, I work in cycles of fifteen minutes. I just have to get through fifteen minutes and we're one step closer to help. But time has a tendency to stand still when you're in agony. Back in the waiting room at A&E, we talk about all kinds of crap as I rock back and forth.

'We can have a dance if you want?' Dan suggests.

I glare at him and don't respond.

By hour two I'm face down on the waiting room floor, arms above my head, with Dan's feet pushing on my shoulders like a weight, trying to keep my head still. There are pools of water around my face from my tears, and the vomit is now nothing but reflux and air. I scramble to my feet and stagger once more towards the nurse at reception. Tears are streaming down my face, snot spews from my nose and my jaw is still convulsing, I'm hysterical and she sees it. Her expression changes from indifference to concern.

'Listen to me,' I slur. 'I'm fucking begging you now. If you don't bring me something to stop this pain, I'm going to hurt myself, I've been thinking about hurting myself for the last hour and I know exactly how I'll do it ... and if I do it'll be all *your* fault. I need some help.'

She looks shocked but surprises me by asking: 'What do you normally ask for?'

'A sledgehammer.'

She waits for me to compose myself. If I want to be taken seriously then sarcasm isn't the right response.

'I've never been in such an extreme situation, but in the past my GP has prescribed diazepam for muscular spams.' I'm lying, not about the diazepam, but about the previous history of muscle spasms. I just know from research and experience that diazepam is used to treat muscle discomfort, and I don't trust her to act if she thinks it's 'just' anxiety.

'I'll see what I can do.'

I know she's trying to rule me out as a 'drug-seeker', and I can't blame her. Diazepam is after all an addictive sedative. But I also don't care about anything except finding a way out of this nightmare.

I go back to the floor. *This is rock bottom, Claire. Literally. You are now literally lying on a floor made of rock!*

'We'll cash in on this, babe,' I hear Dan joke, and once again feel his feet push down on my shoulders. The position might even be sexy, very *Fifty Shades of Grey* dominant, if we both weren't dressed in jogging bottoms and slippers. 'Another thousand words for the book easy!'

I laugh in spite of the situation and it momentarily eases the tension.

A man is rushed past on a gurney and I hear, 'Stab wound to the right shoulder!'

'Oh for fuck's sake!' I groan. 'That's me down the list again!' Now it's Dan's turn to laugh.

'Right!' a stern voice says. 'Claire, I need you to get up off the floor now, please. I have your diazepam.'

I sit bolt upright. Has somebody actually listened to me? The nurse hands me a yellow pill and a disposable cup of water. 'We've found you a bed and we need you to leave this area, please *don't* lie on the floor.' She isn't kind in her tone, but she's reacted to my condition and if it was acceptable to stick my tongue down her throat right then, I would have.

It takes twenty minutes to kick in, but the diazepam does its job. I feel the tension melting from my jaw as the pain finally loosens its hellish grip, the warm ache of tense muscles now relaxed is heaven. I'm lying on a hospital bed, still face down but feeling euphoric. I'm giddy with the relief that only comes after agony. I remain still, not risking movement. With the right medication, pain dissipates. Panic, however, is much harder to shift. I know that diazepam is short-acting. Forty-five minutes tops. It (the panic) is waiting, just waiting for the first twinge of pain to return. The first signs of danger. When pain and panic entwine it's a brutal combination.

After yet another hour in A&E a doctor finally walks into the cubicle where I'm camped out and I feel an immediate rush of relief.

As expected, the pain has crept back, along with all of the previous symptoms and I'm holding my head still with my hands. The doctor is in her late twenties, I'd say, with clear, olive-coloured skin, and dark glossy hair tied in a low ponytail. Her eyes are a piercing green and I'm monetarily stunned by her beauty. She's an angel in a place of discord. *I really should've at least brushed my hair before having a breakdown!* She looks at me quizzically as I explain the pain that I'm experiencing and how long I've been experiencing it for. I notice her frown as she glances at her notes. Once again, I'm struggling to articulate because of the spasms in my jaw.

Before I can finish my sentence, she interrupts: 'Your bloods came back fine, there's nothing wrong with you.'

Dan looks up and I pause. I point to my neck and try to explain once again that I can't stop it from cramping, but she doesn't appear to be concerned and leaves after less than a two-minute consultation. I think I'm in shock – that would explain my lack of reaction. A while later a nurse arrives with another 5mg of diazepam and I take it gratefully, knowing that it will do the trick. However, I also know that the dosage isn't high enough and that it will wear off soon after we get home. So, I bring up the subject of 'aftercare' and my concerns about getting through the weekend until I can see my GP on Monday. 'Could I have a prescription to take home with me in case the spasming returns?' This is more of an insurance policy than anything. Diazepam is, after all, not a medication that should be taken thoughtlessly.

Still, a patient with a broken leg wouldn't be sent home without appropriate aftercare and I expect the bloke who got stabbed was given some sort of pain relief to get him through the days after being discharged.

The nurse considers this thoughtfully. She approaches the doctor and they chat briefly. From the doctor's reaction I don't fancy my odds, so I decide to 'approach the bench' and plead my case directly. 'No,' the doctor asserts without even looking up. 'You're doing this to yourself and if you just calm down it'll go away.' I hear what she said, but I struggle to process the words. I'm an adult, after all, not a child in need of discipline. 'Ten milligrams of diazepam would put a horse to sleep!' she adds.

I keep my cool and I'm proud of that to this day – it would be easy to act irrationally, be offensive or lose my temper. 'Well, as you can see, I'm not a horse,' I respond with as much calm authority as I can muster. 'I'm a woman who has lived with acute anxiety and panic for several years and I know a lot about both the condition and medication.' (I consider suggesting that she google me, but decide that would make me seem like a right dickhead.) 'Also, if a horse has what I have, then I doubt that ten milligrams would barely take the edge off, let alone put it to sleep. I'm experiencing a breakdown, this is *not* normal for me. I don't want to be confrontational, but I do need some help to get me through the weekend, until I can see my regular GP.'

She rolls her eyes, actually fucking rolls her eyes, and in that moment, she's not beautiful any longer. 'You can't have any more.'

I'm exhausted and disillusioned. 'OK, well, can you take these out please?' I nod to the tubes in my left arm.

She looks surprised. 'You're leaving?'

'Yes I am. I don't feel safe here any more and from what I know about my condition, my only other option is to go home and get blind drunk. Or I could always leave here and walk into oncoming traffic. Would you help me then?' I don't wait for her answer and walk back to Dan.

The nurse who attends me is gentle. She removes the tubes and squeezes my hand without saying a word. An act of kindness I'll never forget. She gets it but is powerless to help.

We drive home in silence. It's 3 a.m. Dan is in complete shock, his faith in the NHS shaken to the core. 'I don't understand,' he mumbles. 'Why wouldn't they listen to you?' Dan up until this point lived in a world that idolised its institutions and trusted all of those with power to act correctly and with fairness. It's a rude awakening, especially for a person who hasn't slept.

Once home he collapses into a well-deserved deep sleep. I, however, sneak out of bed, take 150mg of Nytol and grab the only alcohol we have in the house. Dark rum. Ironically, I hate all rum, so this is the cherry on top of a hellish evening.

The panic is hitting in waves, and I can't stop myself from spiralling. *Oh god, this time it's going to kill me. If the pain comes back, I'll kill myself. I can't go back to A&E. The diazepam I took can only last for so long. I can't bear this, I can't. Please leave me alone, please go away. How has this happened? Aren't I supposed to be an expert?* My mind drifts to the knives in the kitchen. I know how to do it. Then, horrified by my own thoughts, I grab the rum and take a swig. I drink long and deep, letting the smoky, sickly sweet liquid ooze down my throat. I gag from the taste. I know that if I don't sedate the part of my brain that's sounding the alarm, then I'm going to do what the police call 'something stupid'. Some people might call my actions disruptive; I call them desperate. I lift the bottle and drink again. I don't realise that I'm crying until the tears drip on to my pyjama bottoms. The heat of the alcohol reaches my empty stomach and pools there soothingly. Sitting in the dark on the living room floor in my new home, I wait in silence for my amygdala to be sub-dued. *Go to sleep now*, I plead. *Please go to sleep*. It takes ten minutes and half a bottle, but it starts to work.

The last time I found myself in this situation, champagne was my rescuer and I sat alone in the dark all night. This time, however, I decide to ring my dad. A strange decision on my part, as we've been going through a difficult patch. Having similar personalities means that we clash. I haven't spoken to him in well over a month, neither of us having a desire to reach out and lacking the humility to do so, but I know he'll pick up. Out of everyone in my life, when I call him, he always picks up, even though he's currently based in Germany and they're an hour ahead. It's five in the morning for him now.

'Dad ... I've had another breakdown and I want to die. I'm so scared.'

I hear the light in his bedroom go on immediately. 'Oh bloody hell, OK.' His Bolton accent is immediately reassuring. 'What's happened?'

We talk for over two hours and in my rum-and-Nytol-induced stupor I honestly can't tell you what we spoke about. But I know he made me feel safe, that he tells me he has all the time in the world to chat, that I'm not a burden, and that we'll get things sorted.

The next thing I remember is waking up on the couch, a concerned Dan hovering over me.

Given my dosage of Nytol and the empty bottle of rum on the floor, I'm lucky to wake up at all. The lure of sleep is heavy and still not finished with me. So, I allow Dan to lead me upstairs to our bed where I succumb again.

When I next wake up I have an appointment with an emergency GP, thanks to Dan and my mum. The doctor in question gives me an emergency prescription of diazepam. It's only three tablets, but the prescription gives me a sense of security.

The next twenty-four hours happen in flashes. I wake up sitting on the couch as my mum feeds me mashed potatoes (I hadn't eaten in two days). She then wakes me again, a few hours later, with her hand in front of my nose to make sure I'm still breathing.

The appointment with my GP on the Monday is a completely different experience. I've known Dr Earnshaw for years. He understands my history and treats me with respect. 'You understand this stuff better than anyone,' he says, 'let's discuss your options.' I explain what happened and I also explain my disgust at using alcohol to help take the edge off the symptoms. Rather than berating me, he says, 'This isn't your fault. You've been blindsided by your illness. Wine is OK in the short term, don't beat yourself up. Just focus on the short term.'

I leave with a sick note, beta-blockers and sleeping tablets to ensure that I get back into a healthy sleeping pattern

I feel exhausted, but I know that I won't relax without some form of sedation. My amygdala was on high alert.

Panic has a knack for making the individual feel as though they're stuck in a vortex that will never end; they worry that they'll always feel as afraid or uncomfortable as they do in *that* moment. Think of it like a whirlwind, stopping any thoughts beyond 'Oh fuck, we're fucked!'

As a basic concept, fear is intolerable, something that a person will do almost anything to distance themselves from.

In the initial weeks after my recovery, I lived in fear of 'the pain' returning and became obsessed with every twinge or movement in my jaw. It held me hostage.

I took to wearing a huge pink scarf from H&M at all times, and smothered my neck in Deep Heat. Personally, I'm not against short-term placebo tactics, although I think people hated the smell!

The thought that there is 'nothing anyone can do to help' with regard to mental illness triggers immediate despair. I'd much rather be lied to: 'OMG of course this chunky scarf will stop the pain from coming back. We actually hand them out on prescription now.'

I couldn't imagine visiting the doctor with a chest infection, only to be told that there's 'a waiting list for treatment', or 'try these tablets, they might work, or they might make you feel worse'. So us 'crazies' do what we can in the short term to provide comfort and security. It's sadly why so many people become reliant on medications such as diazepam, or self-medicate with alcohol or over-the-counter alternatives.

Something I learned over the years is that panic is a shape-shifter. You might figure out how to deal with one symptom and *Boom!* it hits you with another. This isn't a bad thing; the brain, seeking to protect itself, has to adapt and develop additional ways to make us stop. In this instance, it was crippling jaw pain and spasming.

On the third day of my breakdown, I caught sight of myself in a mirror once again.

My eyes were hooded and dull. Huge purple circles rested under them, along with broken blood vessels. I was pale and my lips lacked any pigment. I held my hands up and they trembled like an alcoholic in the early days of detox. *You're killing yourself,* I realised dully. *Not immediately, but blow by blow you're destroying your body. I don't know what more I have to do to make you stop*. I'd never thought of it that way. My brain hurting me in order to make me stop. Was that what the pain in my jaw was? I didn't take heed of the migraine or partial blindness after all. Maybe it had resorted to desperate measures.

Self-care is tricky, it's hard, not to mention time-consuming. It doesn't come naturally to most adults. We think it's an innate response, or a necessity, but really, it's an inconvenience. Staring at my decaying form that day, I finally accepted this. I needed to take rational, pre-planned steps to maintain my wellbeing, rather than presuming that this instinct would kick in naturally.

But what steps could I take exactly?

I read *The Compassionate Mind Guide to Overcoming Anxiety*, by Dennis D. Tirch. I knew by this point, that I had a VERY sensitive amygdala, one that could be triggered easily. However, Tirch also claims that humans have an innate self-comfort system. We don't have anything overtly defensive to protect us like claws or fangs, we instead rely on strong communal bonds that are reinforced by comforting behaviour. As kids, we need our parents to soothe and encourage us when we learn new skills and develop strength. This soothing triggers the release of endorphins and the feel-good hormone oxytocin, which shut down the defence (fight-or-flight) system.

I admit that I'd flirted with the idea of self-compassion over the years, yet I'd never really committed to it. It all sounded a little on the hippy-dippy side, whereas I preferred the self-flagellators camp; *Do better, you stupid bitch!* That sort of thing. But as a result of my situation, I was willing to give compassion another try.

After faffing about with various exercises, I ended up adapting one from the new-wave behaviouralists: picture a child who is afraid or anxious and comfort them. Tell them that everything is going to be OK and it's not their fault. Instead of a child, I used my own reflection in the mirror. I'd been horrified by how ill and vulnerable I looked. Who the fuck was going to save me from myself if not me?

Listen, I said out loud, *I PROMISE it's going to be OK. You're not well at the moment and that isn't your fault. We need to rest for a few weeks and let everything else go. You're an incredibly strong and brave person who just went off track a bit. But you need to accept that you need help, you can't do this alone any more.*

There was something magnetic about the eye contact. It made me listen and accept my situation. Saying the words out loud also gave them gravitas.

In his book, *Love Yourself Like Your Life Depends On It,* Kamal Ravikant deploys a similar trick to communicate self-compassion. 'I started telling myself, I love myself. A thought I would repeat again and again. First lying in bed for hours, repeating to myself *I love myself, I love myself, I love myself.*' I didn't expect this approach to resonate with my natural cynicism, but his reasoning intrigued me. Thoughts after all trigger emotions, so I decided to give this a shot when I found my mind wandering. 'What if you don't believe that you love yourself? Doesn't matter. Your role is to lay down the pathways, brick upon brick, reinforce the connections between the neurons. The mind already has a strong wiring for love. The body knows it well. It knows that love nurtures, that love is gentle, that love is accepting. It knows that love heals.'

Basically, fake it until the sentiment becomes real. I replaced 'you stupid bitch', with 'I love you'. I still do this when I can't sleep, or when I'm feeling vulnerable.

*

In the following weeks I allowed people to help me. Dan took over the business side of things. He contacted my agent, my editor and other professional contacts. My instincts were screaming at me to do this myself, but each time I felt the urge to take over, I was reminded of the vulnerable creature in the mirror who needed to make some changes.

I let my mum cook for me, rather than insisting I do it myself. She took me out on walks for fresh air and even tucked me up in bed at night. It was nice, and made me feel safe.

I organised nightly phone calls with all of my closest friends as I found talking helpful in the evenings. Talking about really random shit too, such as: 'Who would win in a fight, a kangaroo or a gorilla?' Or 'If you had to shag either Boris Johnson or Donald Trump, like you HAD to, to save the world, who would it be?' Talking helps, it bonds us.

I let my parents pay for things, which I normally rejected out of pride. Food, drinks, £100 in Hobbycraft to keep me distracted!

I reached out to the mental health community via social media. This of all things was the hardest. I worried that it might damage my career or reputation. I was, after all, a supposed 'expert'. But the wave of support was phenomenal. After all, nobody understands a panic attack like somebody who has experienced one. Where the limited government services failed me, social media not only picked up the slack, but shone. As a community, the mental health world understands how to comfort one another. The freedom to be 'crazy' is liberating.

As I write this now, I'm day ninety into my recovery and feel better than I have in a long time. I do the 'mirror talk' three nights a week, or whenever I'm having a bad moment.

I'm learning to take things in my stride, rather than fixating on every bump and setback. When you stop striving for 'complete recovery', or aiming to feel only 'happy', the pressure eases.

Panic attacks link back to time. When I think of panic attack relief, I think of time, as in letting the seconds pass by and making yourself as comfortable as possible while they do. This is something that I'll come back to repeatedly in this book. Time eases panic. Every attack will end, because they always do. If happiness, youth and *Game of Thrones* don't last forever, then neither can a panic attack. FACT.

A little side note on A&E

What I've established about A&E literally derives from its name: 'Accident & Emergency'. As in, they treat people in danger of dying. (Literally and quite right too.)

Based on my own experience, my non-medical expert advice would be to avoid A&E unless you believe your life to be in danger. E.g. with a physical injury, or if you're experiencing suicidal thoughts. Staff on duty don't give a shit about your comfort. (I say this from a place of respect.) It's their job to keep you alive if you're in peril, not to comfort you. You do, however, deserve an appropriate consult-ation and to be treated with respect from all members of staff.

From experience and research, I've found that mental illness is not generally prioritised over physical injury, unless there's a designated mental health liaison nurse assigned to the hospital and they are on duty. So, again, I'd advise against going to A&E, unless you require a specific kind of medication, or are feeling suicidal. In a nutshell, if you can take two Nytol, get in the bath and make it through the night by chatting complete shit on the phone to a Samaritans volunteer, then that's a better bet than sitting in A&E. If you're in need of helpful resources, head to page 239.

I'm not saying it's fair, but I also don't like the thought of anyone spending four hours on a stone floor!

CHAPTER 2

What Does a Panic Attack Feel Like?

December 2012

*S*omething's wrong, I know I say this a lot, but I REALLY mean it this time. Shit, this is bad, VERY bad. I continue walking, ignoring the voice in my head. We've had a volatile relationship at the best of times and today is no different.

It's just nerves, I hiss, while entering the meeting room and greeting the colleagues who will shortly be interviewing me for a promotion. Taking a seat, I grin manically and faff around with my notes. I've been prepping for this moment for over a week, twenty-eight hours to be exact, and all I have to do is get through the next thirty minutes. Then I can go home, eat that giant stuffed-crust pizza and drink all the wine required to transport me back to my happy place. **The wine flows freely there, and the bath water never gets cold. There's a steady supply of true crime podcasts, Pinterest boards dedicated to 1930s dress silhouettes, eighteenth-century military jackets and Kurt Cobain's love of knitwear (my style is changeable). Oh, and a nice dose of cute dogs being naughty in YouTube compilations. If it's been a particularly good month, there's champagne from ALDI too, or at least Cava. It's cracking!**

I suck in my stomach and straighten up, as I always do to regain control, but this time I notice that my arms feel heavy and my mouth is dry.

It's fine, it's fine, I whisper again, shaking my head and attempting to take a deep breath, but the air catches in my throat. I inhale again, without success. Instead my lungs tighten and burn as I try to force the air down. Surely, one deep, satisfying breath would sort everything out. So why is my body rejecting it? What's wrong? The fear that started as a tingle mutates into a roar.

Then *IT* happens. A warm, not unpleasant tingling sensation flows through my body like an electric current. I feel it firing down my legs and to the very ends of my fingertips. When it reaches my chest, everything erupts. My heart isn't just beating any more, it's pounding, punching violently at my ribcage, demanding attention. Have I been punched in the chest and not realised? I blink furiously as my eyesight blurs and my lungs contract even more. *Please, please stop.* My stomach gurgles and twists uncomfortably as sweat pours down my back. I haven't lost control of my bowels since I was a baby, but I'm not so confident now. But most of all is the overwhelming feeling that something is VERY wrong.

You're dying. Fuck, you're having a heart attack, or is this a stroke? You're going crazy, you are right this second losing your mind. It's game over. Get out.

When the second wave strikes, I feel detached from my body, suspended in a state of numb terror.

This is it. This is the end. Nothing will ever be the same.

I don't care about anything any more. All the work I've put into preparing for this meeting, my job, my career, money, future: it all seems insignificant next to a burning desire to get out of the room and run.

What happens next confuses me. Sure, it fits with my ridiculous back catalogue of weird reactions over the years, but still. In this moment, in the interview room, I stand up and this sentence comes out of my mouth:

'I have the norovirus ... and must leave AT ONCE!'

I deliver this statement in the purest Queen's English which, considering I'd never used the phrase 'at once' in my entire working life *and* the fact I'm from Bolton, is a surprise for everyone. I've gone from saying 'All right?' as a greeting to bidding them farewell like I'm Jane Austen.

Still, in all its *'oh my god, we're dying'* glory, that is what my brain does to get me out. This is the great escape plan, a line that could have come from a Regency costume drama.

I don't wait for their reaction. I bolt from the room and I run. Down the corridor, the stairs, past the two snooty middle-aged blondes on reception (why are they always so fucking snooty? Receptionists that is, not blondes) and all the way down the street. I have completely lost control and it is terrifying.

The first question to surge into my head is 'What just happened?' Or rather, 'What the fucking fuck just happened?!' Am I dying? Am I losing my mind? Why is my body reacting this way? All reasonable questions to ask. The brain is after all hard-wired to look for cause and effect. Or, as Paul Li, a lecturer of cognitive science at the University of California, Berkeley, explains: 'The parasympathetic nervous system works with the rational part of our brain to identify a situation and then stabilise the sympathetic nervous system.'[1] (Basically, the panic part.)

Therefore, when there isn't an obvious external cause, as with panic, we freak out (for want of a better phrase). But I'm getting ahead of myself.

I run for around forty minutes, about halfway home, before my uncomfortable footwear forces me to hail a black cab that I absolutely can't afford. Luckily, even though I'd thought I was dying, I'd still managed to grab my handbag on my way out of the office (the rational part of my brain was apparently lurking in there somewhere!). *You might be losing your shit, Claire, but you still need your purse.* I climb inside the first taxi that stops, immediately missing the relief that all the running had provided. 'I don't know whether I want to go home or to the hospital!' I blurt. No doubt used to emotional outbursts, the driver takes it all in his stride.

I didn't realise it at the time, but that ride was the beginning of my journey with panic attacks . . . and boy was it going to be a bumpy one.

To say that the days (and nights) that followed were rotten, would be like labelling the coronavirus an unfortunate case of the sniffles. Terror, and I mean true terror, is like free-falling down a black hole without an end in sight. At least if I had a massive heart attack then I'd die, and it'd be over. In contrast, this torture was endless, I was experiencing cycle after cycle.

I truly believed that I'd ruined my life by 'losing control' in front of other people that day. It's acceptable to do that sort of shit alone, locked in the bathroom sobbing, but not in public. Everybody knew that. In my mind, I'd caused this massive scene and 'outed' myself as a lunatic, someone who should never be trusted.

As the doctor signed me off work for a month and diagnosed 'acute social anxiety and panic attacks', I asked her what a panic attack was. She quoted from what sounded like a medical textbook in response: 'the person feels as though they're about to die or lose their sanity', all said in the breeziest of manners and without looking up. I waited for the inevitable *we'd better call the white van* comment, or *I'm afraid you'll never be able to work again.* But she was completely nonchalant as she wrote a prescription for medication that: 'might have an effect' and recommended that I rest for a month. I felt confused, frustrated even.

'You don't understand,' I told her. 'I completely lost it in front of some very senior colleagues. Then I ran all the way down the Strand in heels sobbing. People witnessed this. It was very serious.'

She remained silent.

'That evening, I was rolling around the floor in my flat screaming. I felt like my chest was about to explode.' I started crying again, willing her to take me seriously.

'Yes.' She nodded. 'Panic attacks can be distressing. We'll see how you are in two weeks.'

At this point I would have welcomed the white van and a stay in a secure unit. Any reaction was better than nothing at all. Panic attacks couldn't be as standard as she was suggesting, I refused to believe it. They were so much more than merely 'distressing'. How could she undercut everything that I'd gone through in the last seventy hours with a single adjective? I was out of control and dangerous. Couldn't she see that? At any moment my heart could explode, or I'd drive my car off a bridge (not that I'd allowed myself to drive and I didn't live near any bridges).

Was I the only one who'd experienced such violent symptoms? Or did I have the monopoly? At the time, I felt completely alone and isolated. No one I knew had ever had a panic attack. It wasn't something that came up in standard conversations. In fact, the only reference I had to panic attacks was 'the brown paper bag' parody deployed in films when a character is 'freaking out'. But such scenes always looked so comical, nothing like my experiences.

What I didn't know then was that panic attacks strike a significant number of us, and manifest in different ways. I've asked several people to describe their first panic attack to show you that we are definitely not alone:

I was sitting at my desk at work and my heart started to pound. My breathing became laboured and my chest tightened.

I was taking small gasps of air, and there seemed to be less and less oxygen in the atmosphere.

I became very frightened and eventually called 111. I believed I was having a heart attack. My friend drove me to the nearest A&E and I was rushed through for an ECG. I couldn't believe the results when they said nothing was physically wrong with me. No one explained to me that I was having a severe panic attack, instead telling me that it was 'all in my head'.

– Harriet

It was Valentine's Day and I was on my way to visit a girl, who I'll call 'Mia'. I'd been dating Mia for a few months and she was kind enough to invite me to her birthday, at a pub near Finsbury Park.

As I approached the pub, I was astonished by how large it was. It was an almighty fortress with raucous crowds spilling in and out of the doorway, which in turn was guarded by two intimidating bouncers. Even though it was a wintry evening, I was sweltering under my coat. I felt my heart pound heavy against my chest, almost in time with the rhythmic bass thumping the pub windows. I felt a tightening in my chest. It suddenly felt as though my body was being dragged as far away from the pub as possible.

I took a seat at a nearby bus stop to try and collect my thoughts. After several deep breaths, I decided to loop around the block once more in a feeble attempt to wear my anxiety out but as soon as the pub loomed back into view, the streets began to spin and I once again found myself trundling straight past the pub and back towards the bus stop.

Suffice to say this routine continued several times over, in what can only be considered the world's most frustrating marathon. The more laps I completed, the more disorientated I felt, and my hands were shaking harder than I'd ever seen them. After checking the time, I realised I had spent over an hour simply trying to enter the venue. I felt utterly humiliated. My instinctual thought was to give up, go home and crawl straight into bed.

– Julian

I lay in the dark, amid Spice Girls posters and an army of fluffy teddies, feeling like the ceiling was crushing down on my chest, pleading with Baby Spice and favourite teddy 'Minky' to help me remember how to breathe.

I was stubborn from an early age, so there was no crying out for help, just hours ticking by, while I contorted myself into differing positions to try to stop my chest from closing up, clutching my chest as I rode the waves of pure and utter terror.

In the years that have passed, I don't reach out to Baby Spice for help (Minky is still around though!) but no matter the combination of pills and therapy and time, those vivid feelings – my body being broken apart by what I can only describe as a huge force of impending doom, the constricting throat that morphs itself into a tiny thin emergency supply mode that isn't pumping nearly enough oxygen into the body, the heart palpitations, the stomach pains, the brain's need to anchor itself on to something – will only make you panic more.

– **Amy**

I was on a very crowded tube during rush hour and felt as though I was floating through water. I couldn't hear anything, and I couldn't catch my breath. I thought I might faint and suddenly felt irrationally angry about how many people were in the carriage and forced my way off. Once on the platform I paced frantically, trying to calm down. I couldn't really explain what was happening, just that something felt 'wrong'. I ended up being an hour late for work and felt jumpy all morning.

– **Mark**

To describe these stories as merely 'distressing' is beyond insulting.

So, *what the fuck* is a panic attack exactly? What is this 'beast' that strikes without warning and fills us with terror? And why do so many in the medical profession not take the devastating effects seriously?

My journey towards answering these questions began with a discovery in January 2013, when I googled: 'what not to do during a panic attack'. Nothing I'd tried so far was doing any good. (Oh, you know, just the standard healthy stuff: fighting it, ignoring it, calling myself a *stupid bitch* etc.) If anything, the attacks were lasting longer. So, I resorted to the internet. Along with the usual masses of medical garb and ads for therapy, I discovered Dr David Carbonell, the uncrowned king of panic (and who shall be referred to A LOT in this book). I devoured his website The Anxiety Coach and bought his book *The Panic Attacks Workbook* immediately.

Had I finally found someone who explained the panic experience with emotive language and understanding? *Panic is a devious, insidious trick that can make you feel like a prisoner in your own life.* (Page 8.) Ding ding! Now we're talking. Or, *when you suspect that your life or sanity is on the line, you need something other than positive self-talk to help you.* Carbonell provided the forthright 'panic' insight that I was searching for.

The second great discovery occurred in February 2013, on a Sunday morning, when I tripped over my own feet (this happens a lot) and nearly fell head first downstairs. As I tripped, however, my left hand snatched the bannister, stabilising my legs and preventing any more movement. I didn't plan on reaching for the bannister, it just happened. I stayed there for a moment, breathing hard, and noticed that my heart was pounding. I felt hot, alert and my eyesight was blurry. I was also aware of the spark of fear that had jolted through my body, the evidence of which was still visible in my trembling hands. *Danger*, I thought, *I was in danger and both my brain and body reacted before I even had chance to think*. This reminded me of my first panic attack in the boardroom. The symptoms were the same – pounding heart, breathlessness, sweating – yet, I wasn't in any danger. Similarly to tripping on the stairs, in the boardroom my brain reacted as though I needed to grab the bannister. It was trying to defend me.

Could this be the key? In short: **yes**. I mean I could drag it out for the word count, but I fucking HATE people who do that.

The Claire Eastham definition of a panic attack: A primitive and normal reaction to danger, when a person is *not* in danger; they are in fact in a safe or familiar environment. The brain malfunctions and mistakes stress or nerves for a looming threat. The rush of adrenaline that follows is both confusing and terrifying. Not to mention very inconvenient.

I formed this definition after weeks of obsessive research into panic as an inherent defence system, which is triggered by an almond-shaped organ in the brain called the amygdala. If you type 'fight or flight' (or acute stress response) into Google, then you'll most likely be presented with the primitive man analogy and how the fight-or-flight response benefited him in the survival stakes (when there were predators knocking around with bigger teeth than a Tory government). It was first described by American psychologist Walter Cannon in the year 1920. However, all you really need to know about fight or flight is that it's your brain's security system, a defence that springs into action during times of danger. It floods the body with adrenaline and sharpens the senses, thus providing the extra boost to either run away from the threat, fight it, or in my case, reach for the bannister to stop myself from falling downstairs. The phrase 'sympathetic nervous system' is thrown around a lot too, which amuses me. As though this neurological structure is 'terribly sorry' for the inconvenience.

While researching this book, I reached out to the lovely Dr Soph, a modern psychologist with a strong Instagram following. Her object- ive is to 'take therapy out of the therapy room' and she provides sessions via video link.

We talked extensively about the amygdala.

'Your brain has evolved to keep you safe above all else. It is con- stantly on the lookout for danger. Once it finds something potentially dangerous it steps in and initiates the fight-or-flight response. This means it takes away your conscious control of the situation.'

It's the reason why you jump at loud noises or flinch involuntarily when you see a spider on the wall. Your sympathetic nervous system reacts before you even have the chance to think.

I was also fortunate enough to meet with Dr Andrea Reinecke, a senior research fellow and clinical psychologist at the University of Oxford, working on a profound mental health research project with MQ (the charity for which I'm an ambassador). We discussed the sensitivity of the amygdala, the brain's bodyguard: 'Its sole and only purpose is to ensure survival by identifying and reacting to danger. There is no plan B, only a plan A, which is to initiate the fight-or- flight response.'

OK, fine, so panic has a purpose. But what about the literal symp- toms of panic? After yet another panic attack on the Victoria line (the hottest and most stressful of all the underground lines), I take a moment to really pay attention to the symptoms that I'm experien- cing. Pounding heart? Yes, fine. Heavy breathing? OK. But why do I feel the need to shit myself, and how is that going to help me survive? By disgusting a potential predator? Also, what about the sweating and blurred vision, how are they beneficial? These symptoms seemed random and useless. However, I learn from Dr Carbonell that sweat is a classic resistance tactic beneficial to primitive man: 'If you were under attack, your body would want to make itself as slippery as possible to avoid being caught in the predator's grip.' I picture myself as a fish, slipping out from between a cat's paws. I suppose that would be useful. And the shitting thing? 'The body will purge itself in order to eliminate any unnecessary weight. This makes flight easier.' I mean, gross, but I see the logic.

Researching the individual symptoms became addictive. I felt like I was learning about a new superpower with each discovery. Heavy limbs, for example, are a result of the veins retreating deeper into the muscle tissue to reduce blood loss if struck. Oh, and the blurred vision thing? 'The pupils dilate to allow in more light, so we can work out an exit strategy. This can make vision blurry up close.' Thank you very much Sarah Wilson, author of *First, We Make the Beast Beautiful*. Always great to come across another person seeking truth in science.

What I discovered was that the random and seemingly illogical symptoms that I experienced during a panic attack not only have an important part to play, but are each customised to aid my survival.

Wow. *Huge* respect to my brain. For the first time in months, I took a moment to appreciate how truly amazing the body is. Even my veins know their job!

What I took from this intense research, is that while 'fight or flight' is the traditional response to danger, a panic attack is the result of this response being triggered in error. For example, when I nearly fell down the stairs, I didn't question why my heart was pounding or why my mouth was dry. There was a clear explanation for these symptoms, and the adrenaline produced by 'fight or flight' was being put to good use. However, when I felt them during a 'normal' situation, such as a meeting or on the tube, I felt confused. When there is no danger and you don't make use of the extra adrenaline, the brain becomes distressed.

What follows is a battle of wills between the rational brain and the amygdala, which nine times out of ten, the amygdala wins. Why? Well, think about it this way, the brain's desire *not* to die is stronger than the urge *not* to look like a tit in front of John from HR by legging it out of the room. Dr Paul MacLean writes about the 'three brains' and how they grew on top of each other: *the frontal lobe, the lizard and the cortex.*[2] The frontal lobe is the emotional part, concerned with core urges such as sex, love and danger. (For this reason, psychiatrist Dr Walter Freeman sought to cure a number of 'hysterical' women back in the 1950s by knocking out the frontal lobe during an 'ice pick lobotomy'.[3]) It also happens to be the strongest of the brains. The cortex is the rational part and grew last, thus making it the weakest.

Not exactly a fair fight then. Yet, it does clarify beautifully not only why a panic attack occurs, but also why it's so hard to control.

The pre-symptoms

It came out of the blue!

In the six months that followed my first attack, I was very certain of this statement. Panic strikes out of nowhere: one minute I'm fine and the next I'm hurled into a hurricane of terror. Part of the fear was always the 'not knowing'. How could I control something that didn't follow a logical pattern? As David Carbonell explains, 'The majority of symptoms are immediate and intense, a pounding heart for example, there's a reason we call it an attack.'[4]

The first flicker of doubt came after a conversation with a friend who I hadn't seen in a while. 'How are you sleeping these days?' she asked. 'You were all over the place the last time I saw you.'

This confused me. She was referring to our last meet-up, which was around three months before my first attack. We'd been having drinks at a mutual friend's birthday. 'You hadn't been sleeping more than four hours a night.' She squeezed my hand softly. 'You also mentioned terrible stomach cramps. Did that turn out to be IBS? It could be dairy, you know, or maybe alcohol poisoning!' She laughed and I tried not to take offence. Sure, I liked a drink, but no more than the next young professional. 'I still can't believe how much you can put away. Three drinks and I'm out!'

I bristled. 'Why were you focusing on how much I was drinking anyway?' It came out more like a bark than a question and I tried to soften the blow with a laugh. We both knew it was forced.

She blushed and looked uncomfortable. 'Don't you remember? You told me that it was the only thing that kept the demons quiet.'

Butterflies in the stomach is a well-known saying. Sure, the name isn't very scientific, but the concept is solid. Research has proven that the digestive system is in sync with a person's thoughts and emotions. (More on this in chapter eleven.) After all, the adrenal glands are found in the gut, which produce adrenaline and cortisol. Butterflies are an indication that the fight-or-flight response has been activated in some capacity. It's cute, right? Nothing to worry about.

But what about stomach piranhas? Reflecting on the period before my nervous breakdown, I'd been having trouble with my stomach. Nausea, cramping and diarrhoea several times a week. At one point I even had a food intolerance test done, certain that I was being poisoned by something.

It turns out that my brain was trying to tell me something, communicating via a variety of uncomfortable symptoms. Along with stomach piranhas, there was insomnia, a persistent dry mouth, a tremor in my hands, restlessness and irritability. I ignored them all, or rather, drowned them in wine, along with the little voice that hissed: *something's wrong.*

Few people were willing to talk about anxiety at that time, let alone panic attacks. The lack of public conversation was a problem for everyone. As author Sarah Wilson beautifully puts it: 'Anxious behaviour is rewarded in our culture. Being highly strung, wound up and so busy has cachet.'[5] I didn't want to come across like the person who 'couldn't cope' with life, so I buried how I was feeling, and wine certainly helped. However, knowing what I do now about panic and anxiety, this was the equivalent of trying to cover an erupting volcano with tissue paper! Still, with so little advice available, the majority of which being inaccessible to non-medical staff, why should I have known better?

In December 2012, on that fateful day in the boardroom, panic hadn't struck out of the blue like an unknown assailant. It had been sending polite notes, advising of its impending arrival. Like any condition, it all comes down to reading the signs. For example, 'Sore throat, cough and a runny nose?' Then you probably have a cold.

In the years that followed, I put something similar together, to help me not only recognise a panic attack, but also the evolutionary benefit of most of the symptoms. I still carry it with me most days.

1. **Heart palpitations** – caused by adrenaline to aid physical exertion
2. **Hyperventilating** – occurs because my breathing has become shallow and rapid, in response to the extra adrenaline
3. **Dizziness** – lack of oxygen, because of aforementioned shallow breathing
4. **Nausea or the urge to void bowels** – my body is trying to make me lighter, so I can run faster
5. **Sweating** – slippery skin is harder for predators to grab
6. **Heavy/numb limbs** – the veins are retreating into my muscles. Less chance of bleeding out if I'm attacked by a tiger
7. **Blurry vision** – my pupils have dilated to allow more light in and look for an escape

Late at night on Boxing Day 2019

I had a horrendous panic attack. I was the only one in the house still up, binge-watching *RuPaul's Drag Race* on Netflix, and the symptoms of the attack caught me completely off guard. *Something's wrong, you need to wake people up.* I felt dizzy and my chest was tight. As usual, panic didn't pull any punches. The symptoms were violent enough to momentarily doubt my panic attack education. *THIS is different, you're suffocating. Are you really willing to die just to prove a point?* I frantically paced around my parents' living room, clutching my chest and sweating furiously. *I don't want to die, please, I don't want to die.*

I was afraid, yet stubborn enough to pull out my handy pre-written panic attack list and look over the symptoms. Pounding heart? Check. Heavy limbs? Check. Stomach cramps? Check. Sweaty? Check.

I then walked to the bathroom and looked at myself in the mirror. Calmly, I said out loud, 'It's OK, you know what this is. It's a panic attack. Nothing bad is going to happen. You're safe.' Panic pushed back a few times, testing my resolve: *you need to go to hospital now!* I removed my slippers and felt the cool of the bathroom tiles on my feet. Turning on the tap to distract my brain further, I repeated: 'It's OK. The fight-or-flight response has been triggered by mistake. There's no danger here, you're safe. This might feel horrendous, but it isn't dangerous. It's a panic attack and it will pass in time.'

I stood there for a good five minutes, soothing myself. When the symptoms of the attack lessened, I made a cup of tea and I went back to RuPaul. 'If you can't love yourself ... how the heeeell you gonna love somebody else?' AMEN to that!

Understanding what was happening to my body had put me back in the driving seat. Turns out that knowledge really is power.

CHAPTER 3

The Big Trick: Why Panic Attacks Happen

> [Trigger Warning: This chapter contains graphic
> depictions of violence.]

The girl sliced through her arm with an electric carving knife. It roared and then strained as the blade collided with bone. Blood sprayed in every direction and in seconds her face was completely covered in gore. She didn't make a sound, shock clearly overwhelming her urge to scream.

An extreme course of action perhaps, but given her circumstances, I think it was for the best. It's probably what I'd have done too, if a demon was trying to steal my soul by biting my arm. (I think it was a venom thing. The plot wasn't concrete.)

The people to my left cringed and covered their eyes defensively. I was at the Odeon cinema in Leicester Square, watching the remake of *Evil Dead*, and I was about to have an epiphany with Butterkist popcorn stuck between my teeth.

The demon made another on-screen appearance and everybody screamed, including me.

My heart beat faster, and I squirmed, feeling afraid. I imagined myself being stuck in that same cabin with those other ridiculous twenty-something-year-olds. I mean seriously, a secluded cabin in the woods. I'm not surprised that the son of the Devil turned up. It was either going to be that or an axe murderer ... or maybe an ancient inbred family who survived on the blood of virgins. 'I can smell your filthy soul!' It hissed at the poor girl, who by now was babbling something at her blockhead of a boyfriend. The fear became so intense that my brain froze in response to the distress, then begged me to leave the cinema. Which was silly when I thought about it, because nothing bad was really going to happen to me. The demon couldn't physically reach through the screen and force me to cut my arm off too.

So why was I so afraid? Why couldn't my brain establish between the two realities? Then the penny dropped, like the proverbial lead weight. *Fuck ... the feeling that I'm experiencing right now is just like a panic attack. Yes, I'm terrified and feel like I'm in danger, but it's false. The danger isn't real.*

At this point, I should mention that the plot had got completely out of hand ... blood rained from the sky, nail guns and a self-made defibrillator were in use. Standard horror film shit. Yet, I couldn't give less of a shit because I was excited about my realisation: **a panic attack is a trick and the symptoms it produces are just a sign that the brain has been fooled into feeling afraid**. Just like a horror film.

In the weeks following my nervous breakdown and first panic attack, I spent a great deal of time asking why. Why was this happening to me? Why was I experiencing panic attacks on a daily basis and why couldn't I control them? All the usual self-pitying stuff, and yet instinctive. As Einstein said: 'The important thing is not to stop questioning. Curiosity has its own reason for existence.' The curiosity in me was on fire.

I absorb things better when I understand why they occur. Don't we all? The apple went brown BECAUSE the outer peel was broken, and the air got to it. Understood. You have to stop at a red light BECAUSE it's the law. Sorted. You got the equation wrong BECAUSE you forgot to divide by ten. No problem. As psychologist David Berlyne highlights, when humans encounter situations that conflict with our previous understanding, or when we feel that there is a gap created by uncertainty, we are driven to seek answers that will reduce the unpleasant sensation.[1] Basically, we feel unnerved if we don't understand. Think of it like an itch that we can't scratch. Tyler Tervooren, founder of Riskology, believes that 'why' is the most important question in the whole universe. 'The potential that it carries when it's asked is immense and the knowledge and empowerment it provides when it's answered is unmatched by any other force.'[2]

I was routinely told that there was technically nothing *wrong* with me, yet I refused to believe it. If I was feeling this bad, then there must be a problem. Conventional or not.

Doctors and medical staff would ask: *have you been under a lot of pressure recently?* My honest answer was always: *no more than usual.* I could understand my breakdown if I was being bullied, or financially supporting a family of five, but I wasn't. I was just the same as every other 25-year-old. Working full-time, living in the capital and getting by on the wage that was awarded to me.

After yet another frustrating conversation with an individual in the medical profession, I decided to take matters into my own hands.

I should point out that in 2013 there wasn't anywhere near as much information available on panic attacks as there is now, so I spent a lot of time scrolling through medical journals and academic studies.

Thanks to the incident when I nearly fell downstairs, I knew that panic was a physical response to danger, but what else was going on? I researched the amygdala, the part of the brain responsible for the 'fight-or-flight' response extensively. It's worth pointing out that during my research I found an article titled: 'Can I have my amygdala removed?' The idea being that having this part of the brain destroyed would make a person fearless. I laughed out loud, thinking this to be an urban legend, but no, it isn't. The removal of the amygdala is called amygdalotomy and is a well-known procedure in both the USA and Japan, first pioneered in 1939 by Heinrich Klüver and Paul C. Bucy. It is said that up to 500 patients received the operation throughout the 1960s. I won't lie, at various points in my recovery I've looked into this operation. However, further investigation revealed that rather than to reduce fear or anxiety, this procedure was used primarily to treat severe aggression, or epilepsy.

The most famous patient to experience an amygdalotomy naturally was 'patient SM', a 44-year-old woman with a rare condition called Urbach–Wiethe disease, or lipoid proteinosis. The condition causes parts of the brain to harden and waste away and this destroyed patient SM's amygdala. After the destruction, researcher Justin Feinstein led a study that determined her ability to feel fear. During the study Feinstein and his team attempted to scare SM with a variety of standard triggers, e.g. spiders, snakes (which she previously claimed to hate), jump scares, etc. Yet, the findings were as follows: 'Haunted houses, where monsters tried to evoke an avoidance reaction, instead evoked curiosity.'[3] She also enjoyed holding a snake, exclaiming 'this is so cool!' She found that not even horror films had an impact, explaining that she 'felt nothing' during the most frightening scenes.

This is not to say that patient SM lacked an understanding of fear as a concept. Or lost the ability to feel other emotions such as happiness or sadness. With regard to the horror films she accepted that other people might be scared by what she watched. On the other hand, studies also showed that she had issues detecting danger. For example, the team noted that she'd happily stand a foot away from complete strangers, far closer than most people would be comfortable with. In 1994, she was also held at knifepoint in a park local to her house. Rather than cowering, she argued with her assailant. The man eventually let her go and she walked away calmly.[4]

I mean, this is a badass story and all, but fuck! Not only would I have offered the nice knife man ALL of my belongings right down to my knickers, I expect I would have also avoided all parks, maybe even garden centres too, for the rest of my days!

In this sense, I suppose the good news was that my amygdala was fully operational. It could identify a threat and react accordingly. Great. The bad news was that it behaved like a smoke alarm with a caffeine addiction and was being triggered in situations that were inappropriate. But why?

I knew by this point that I'd been living with undiagnosed social anxiety and stress for the last fifteen years. I treated my reaction to stress like a character flaw, one that could be corrected. I also used my fear of failure as a motivator. The notion being that with hard work and discipline, I could train myself to succeed at anything, or to become any person.

During my master's degree, for instance, I also had a full-time job, and a demanding one at that. I worked at a local law firm on the switchboard. The phones in that place never stopped ringing and apart from my thirty-minute lunch break, I barely had a moment to think.

On one occasion, a rude caller pissed me off so much that I not only disconnected the call but proceeded to unplug the entire switchboard (bear in mind that over 200 people worked in that office), preventing said caller from ringing back. *Genius. That'll show him.* I would've left it unplugged for an hour, except that one of the senior partners came out of his office and commented: 'Is there a problem with the phones? I'm expecting an important call.' I then had to pretend that I was rebooting the system due to a 'technical fault'. Fortunately, he believed me. This is similar to how I'd been dealing with my mental health for years. My amygdala was the busy switchboard that I was trying to ignore. (To this day I'm still surprised that I wasn't fired from that job, or at least disciplined for my attitude!)

Every other student on the course treated the MA as their full-time job, which was the sensible thing to do. Alas, not me, I had to work in order to pay for my higher education, if I wanted to complete it within a year that is. Otherwise, I could've done the course over a two-year period, or simply saved up in advance. Yet, that would've required a certain level of reason and patience that I did not possess. In my mind, I *would* succeed, and I would do it quickly. Success at a young age felt like the ultimate achievement and I was obsessed by pursuing it without really stopping to ask why. After all, wasn't that the message I'd been fed by the media? Even now modern culture fixates on youthful achievement. It's a fetish. As *Guardian* journalist Ammar Kalia writes: 'It seems we increasingly celebrate youthfulness as a marker of success in and of itself; *Teen Vogue*'s Under 21 list began in 2017. This year's cohort includes 11-year-old designer Kheris Rogers and seven-year-old "activist" Havana Chapman-Edwards.'[5]

I recently made friends with a young woman who used to work for Burberry. We bonded over our shared history of needing to be successful at a young age by working for a worldwide 'brand', a company that everyone was aware of and therefore validates us. (Because that's a sign of a secure person, right?) Like my new friend, I lived for moments at parties when someone asked where I worked. 'Me? Oh, I work for X publisher.' I'd beam internally as I answered. *How fucking cool do I sound right now?* Ten seconds of childlike pride (or smugness) in exchange for months of anxiety. Fair trade? NO, in a word. Said friend is now a florist and a very happy one at that.

So, during my MA days I worked all day and studied at night and at weekends. This hectic work schedule is doable for a month, maybe two at a push, but certainly not nine! I developed insomnia and when I did fall asleep, I'd wake up with heart palpitations and gasping for air. Coincidence? No. I now understand that this was my brain warning me. It was a shadow of things to come, which I promptly ignored.

I remember the night before I had to submit my dissertation, I'd been up for forty-eight hours straight and I blacked out at my parents' computer. I woke up twenty minutes later, shaking on the floor. Had I fallen off the chair, had I collapsed? I have no idea. After clambering to my feet, I cursed myself for being *fucking pathetic* and then had a cold shower. It was around 3 a.m.

How I didn't have a heart attack during that period I'll never know. Although I did develop a tremor in my hands, which I still have today. Doctors can't prove for certain what caused it, but I reckon I fried something deep in my circuit board. If we ever meet, ask me to hold my hands out straight and I'll show you.

I thought I'd be euphoric when I submitted that 20,000-word demon paper. I'd done it! What an incredible achievement. I drove for nearly an hour to Preston (or rather my dad drove me, as I could barely function), and handed the precious, laminated bundle over to a mute woman in the admin office. She was eating a bacon sandwich at the time and some of the grease transferred on to the cover page. I didn't expect balloons, but maybe a smile, or a well done. Then again, why should she give a shit?

Surely I should have felt happy? But I didn't, I felt numb. On the journey home my legs were shaking, and I was sweating profusely. Was I hot or cold? I couldn't tell. Dad got me a McDonald's and I spent the day silent on the couch.

That evening I went out to celebrate a close friend's birthday. The shaking in my limbs was getting worse and I started to feel scared. Even though I'd barely taken two sips of Prosecco, I felt drunk and struggled to focus. I feigned a headache and went home at 10 p.m. I was exhausted and yet felt wired. Something was wrong. Why couldn't I relax? My head was a storm of activity and emotion and all I wanted to do was make it stop. I grabbed a bottle of red wine from my parents' cabinet, downed half of it in one go, crawled into bed and promptly passed out. The next thing I knew, my mum was waking me at 6 p.m. the following day to tell me that my tea was ready. I'd been asleep/unconscious all day.

Why didn't I tell anyone about how I was feeling? I honestly don't know. In many ways, I think I was on another planet, separate from my body. It never occurred to me that this level of 'ambition' wasn't normal, or indeed healthy. Besides, it was behaviour that had been rewarded all my life.

Things improved quickly after 'dissertation gate'. I didn't have to study in the evenings any more and I finally had some time for myself. I'd got away with it by the skin of my teeth and everything was quickly forgotten.

Maybe if I'd have stopped there and learned my lesson, things wouldn't have escalated the way that they did.

Fast-forward six months and after months of applications and interviews, I was offered a job in publishing.

To say that my move to London in 2013 was a dream come true is an understatement, not to mention landing a job at one of the biggest publishers in the UK. I'm from a semi middle-class background: my parents work hard, and we never went without, but I had to work if I wanted money. I could never work for free for instance (for the experience, via an internship), or take a year out and ask my parents to pay for acting school/a gap year travelling or whatever. I paid for my education and I have always funded my lifestyle. Although, when you've never known any different, you don't tend to think about it, let alone feel bitter. My work ethic gives me a sense of pride. Or at least it used to, before it began to horrify me.

Breaking into any of the creative industries can be difficult if you don't have financial backup. I spoke about this with Manchester comedian and writer Rachel Fairburn of the popular *All Killa No Filla* podcast. Rachel worked full-time while developing her comedy set and joked that she constantly applied for voluntary redundancy so that she could focus on her writing. 'I don't think people realise how hard it is for a person from a working-class background to work within this [comedy] industry, or any creative industry.' Those from affluent backgrounds, however, can commit to a creative career without the fear of starving to death. Not that I begrudge anyone for being born with a silver spoon in their mouth; who in all honestly wouldn't take advantage of the opportunities afforded them? Not only with regard to money, but relevant connections and contacts too. Still, it's important to acknowledge and celebrate those who aren't as fortunate. For instance, during my internship (at the same publisher), I had to use all of my holiday allowance from my then current job and stay in a hostel that was so cold I slept in my coat most nights. On the flip side I did make friends with Maya who manned the reception in the evenings. She promised not to let any murderers into my dorm, not realising I was being deadly serious. I'll never forget talking to the other intern who excitedly told me about staying at her aunt's flat in Chiswick and how they'd dined at a jazz club the night before. I didn't have the heart to tell her that I'd spent the night in bed, eating cornflakes straight from the box and reading one of the proof copy YA novels I'd been given.

I was excited to move to London, but greatly underestimated the impact that such a change would have on me. I didn't know anyone and had little experience of living independently.

This was my first 'proper job' and the start of my career. I was so excited to be there, but terrified that I would somehow fuck up and lose everything. It's amazing how similar fear and excitement are. Barry McDonagh, author of *Dare*, believes that a person can actually switch panic to excitement with the right tools. Rather than feeling dread when the early symptoms of panic start, mentally scream, 'Yes, this is great, I want more!' I must admit, I've tried this myself a few times and it can be beneficial, with practice. *Yes! I love this rollercoaster. I'm not shitting myself at all!* If you catch it at the right moment, you can flip the switch, so to speak.

The department I worked in was incredibly intimidating and I was in awe of every person. They were accomplished, had extensive experience in the industry and seemed to burst with confidence. They also seemed to know each other from previous positions. I felt the pressure to prove myself quickly.

From conversations with other colleagues at events, Twitter rants and various online articles (back then), I established that two years was the maximum that one should stay in an entry-level job. Any longer than that and you risk being overlooked.

I've never been good at just coasting along, trusting fate to take me where I'm supposed to be. The idea that I'm not in control physically makes me itch. (Control is a key theme that I'll reference frequently in this book.) 'Go with the flow?' Nah, I'd rather grab the flow by the balls! Because of this, I've always found having goals to be comforting; having something to aim for helps to anchor me. However, somewhere along the way the goal became a cross and I a martyr to it.

By January 2013 I had my new goal. I needed to reach the next career level within two years, and I dived head first into this new project. Not once did I ask myself why. As in 'why' do I need to get to the next level? Why did I want to? Why was it so important? I think I was scared to entertain questions like that. They'd force me to open doors that had been firmly bolted shut. *You have incredibly low self-esteem and value what others think more than your own wellbeing and happiness,* for example. Or, *because if you don't achieve X then what is the point of YOU? You hate yourself and your achievements are the only things that define you. They're the only thing that you can control.*

So, as I said, firmly ... bolted ... SHUT.

I was aware that besides my short internship, I had practically zero experience in the book industry. A large portion of entry-level publishing jobs were filled by ex-booksellers and I needed to catch up. Product knowledge was vital, e.g. bestsellers, authors, imprints, publishing terminology, etc. Most sane people would've been content to take each day as it comes and learn accordingly. Not me, I morphed into Sandy from *Grease* and sought to change everything about myself at rapid speed. Except, unlike Sandy, I didn't have the pink ladies to help with the transformation. So, I reverted back to the system that had worked so well for me in my academic career: research, intense discipline and hard work to the point of exhaustion. I worked all day and gave myself 'homework' for the evenings. Once again, I was working myself into the ground.

I'm a little embarrassed to admit that jealousy, and the rage that accompanies it, was a huge motivator for me (and if I'm really fucking honest, still is). Nothing creates fire quite like envy. I found it oddly centring. No matter how tired I felt, when someone on my level succeeded, it was as though a whip had been cracked across my back, driving me forward ... and like a whip, it caused damage that developed over time.

I took ten months to break, which happened in that infamous meeting when I experienced my first major panic attack, the one that changed my life. I'd finally gone too far.

The mammoth realisation hit me one afternoon at home, when I was writing my then newly established blog, *We're All Mad Here.*

I knew by that point that my place of work was a trigger. That made sense: I'd had my first attack in that office and everything I'd learned about panic highlighted that a person would feel nervous about entering a place where an attack had happened previously. Yet, writing a blog post, I was at home, safe and alone. I felt jittery initially and my stomach churned as I struggled to breathe deep. *It's OK,* I soothed myself, *you're safe.* After completing a useful breathing technique that I'd learned, I went back to typing. Panic struck again, more intense this time. My vision blurred, my heart hammering in my chest. I stood up quickly, knocking the chair over as I did. I wanted to run; I had an overwhelming urge to run.

Work. It hissed. After years of punishment, my amygdala associated a desk and a computer screen with the most extreme danger. The familiarity of sitting down, knowing that I was going to work, triggered the fight-or-flight response.

Dr Trevor Powell, author of *The Mental Health Handbook*, explains that a panic attack, in simple terms, is 'a reaction to stress', in the same way that a headache or nausea is. However, rather than acknowledging stress and taking measures to reduce it (as we would with physical conditions), people tend to ignore it and hope it will go away. Ignorance was exactly the approach I'd taken for a decade. Is it really surprising that my amygdala took things up a notch?

The work environment became my war zone. Thanks to repeated and prolonged stress, my brain could no longer differentiate between emotional and literal danger.

It happened again at an event and then again in a board meeting. When it happened during a dinner party with some of my boyfriend's friends, I finally understood the pattern.

My amygdala was always looking for the threat, the subtle change in tension. A perplexed look from a colleague was considered as dangerous as a knife, or a closed door was considered a blocked escape route. I could no longer tell the difference between physical and mental harm. Therefore, to be on the safe side, my amygdala initiated the fight-or-flight response as default. When discussing 'manufactured fear and synthetic danger' Dr Carbonell likens the amygdala to a dog that barks too much. 'It's good to have a dog that barks when strangers approach your house. But it's a problem if the dog also barks at the kids next door. The dog needs to be trained. If you have panic attacks, you need training too.' A person who experiences regular panic attacks has an amygdala that essentially barks at everything. This acts as a 'fail-safe' approach to ensure survival.

I felt euphoric when the penny dropped. I wasn't mad and I wasn't dying (at least no faster than anyone else). The office environment was my horror film and now that I truly understood the panic trick, I could take steps to manage it.

'A person may experience discomfort and respond as if it were danger. This is the key to what gives panic its power to terrify you. I like to call it "the panic trick".'[6]

This understanding anchored me. It was a new education, so to speak. Dr Soph is passionate about basic brain education: 'Because people aren't taught from a young age what the fight-or-flight response is, when you start panicking, because you interpret those symptoms as dangerous, the brain then interprets another threat, which ironically is itself and it escalates from there. It's very easy to get stuck in a cycle of panic, especially when you don't have people helping you.'

Wonderful, I'd cracked it! I knew what a panic attack was, and I knew why it happened. The end. I could now hope to alter my plan, give my brain a rest on occasion and continue to surge forward down the path towards great success.

So why did I still feel so unhappy? I thought the dark cloud that had been hanging over me for so long would shift now, like the end of an epic fantasy tale. Yet it didn't. Sadness is a great weight, one that crushes the spirit and eats away at your strength. I felt numb. I felt tired. I felt nothing.

I was seeing a shrink on Harley Street at the time. I figured she must be good due to the famous address – long story short, she wasn't. However, she did make one point that stuck with me. 'Are you aware that you've used the phrase "a dream come true" several times in the last ten minutes when talking about your job?' I blinked, taken back. 'Your voice shifts too, like you're hosting a game show. Who are you performing for?' I felt like I'd been kicked in the stomach by someone wearing Doc Martens. Steel-toed Doc Martens. She was right. This woman was perceptive. Maybe she could fix my brain once and for all? Unfortunately, she then proceeded to call me Sophie and asked if I wanted any Valium.

On the bus home I allowed myself, just for a moment, to venture into a part of my subconscious that I usually kept nailed shut. *She saw straight through you*, it hissed. *You have no idea what you want and no fucking clue who you are.* I flinched and shook my head. There was nothing wrong with my life, I was being ridiculous. Scrambling in my bag for my headphones, I listened to the *Wicked* soundtrack all the way home and then promptly dived into bed.

Things carried on as normal. I went to work, had panic attacks, hung out with friends and paid £7 for a small glass of wine. The emotional weight stayed with me and I tried to ignore it.

I went back to Bolton for another friend's birthday one weekend and naturally stayed at home. Mum had been doing some reorganising and my old desk was littered with prized possessions that were previously squirrelled away in drawers. I smiled, looking at my collection of Horrible History books. I had every single edition and the inside cover bore my name. I also had two books from the Tower of London gift shop that were definitely too advanced for a ten-year-old. I was beyond obsessed with the six wives of Henry VIII, Anne Boleyn in particular. The pages were full of scribbles from when I'd made notes. Kids have been obsessed with weirder things, right? I also had a fixation with the Black Death and smallpox. (Totally still do. Seriously my extensive knowledge of random history shit comes in handy at pub quizzes.)

Next to the history books were multiple notepads, filled with what could be described as the worst short stories in the world. I laughed out loud reading them. I was so sure of my narrative back then. The last entry was dated (yes, I dated my work) August 2000. Feeling suddenly embarrassed by my self-indulgence, I snapped the notepad shut.

A wave of emotion crashed over me. *You know why you're so unhappy? You haven't allowed yourself to be your true self in a decade.* (I know, this is some serious icky self-pitying shit, but stay with me.)

I suspected from a young age that there was something 'off' about me. Yes, yes, so does every dramatic teenager with a sob story, who then completes the stereotype with a nose ring and a tattoo. (I don't have a nose ring.) But seriously, there was indeed something 'off'; I just didn't realise that it was diagnosable. For instance, I spent *a lot* of time in my head, most of which was involuntary. I'd zone in and out at random. This made it hard to follow conversations or focus when someone was talking to me. Questions constantly had to be repeated, causing parents/friends/teachers, etc. to lose their patience. I also really liked my own company, which made me resent forced social interactions. Even now I struggle to function when I spot someone I know in a public place, especially on public transport. It's as though my brain can't cope with that person suddenly appearing in my reality. I flounder and react badly, which normally includes a poor attempt at hiding. (Nine out of ten times, I've already been spotted, which makes things incredibly awkward!)

I'm not a traditional people person. I'm introverted, I get tired easily, and bored quickly. Before big events, either business- or family-related, it's not uncommon for me to drink a shedload of caffeine to physically give me the energy to interact, after which I spend half the following day in bed, exhausted. That's just how I am.

In many ways, I had the exact opposite personality desired for a career in publishing, e.g. enthusiastic, outspoken, confident and good at networking. I'm happy to hold my hands up and say that I wasn't right for the job. I just didn't want to accept this at the time. How did I get it in the first place? Simple. I pretended to be some-body else. I'd been doing this since school, so it was no effort. It's how I bagged my first boyfriend, got my first Saturday job and passed the interview for my MA degree. I suppressed my instincts. It just seemed more tactical than being myself.

I became a robot and a key observer of behaviour. I focused on the things that I 'should' want, rather than what I actually wanted. I was so convinced that I had a defective personality that I no longer deferred to my instincts at all. I couldn't be trusted to take the wheel and I was terrified of being left behind.

Besides, this 'version' of me was very well received, unlike the old one. Bear in mind 'introversion' wasn't really celebrated, so to speak, in the early noughties. Extroversion was favoured, thereby making a bubbly and outgoing personality the goal, especially for women. The more enthusiastic and 'all-knowing' you seemed, the better. Vulnerability was the ultimate taboo.

In her book *Quiet*, Susan Cain argues that in the twentieth century a value of 'character' gave way to 'personality'. Whereby, certain traits became more important to have, whether they're natural to the individual or not. 'The pressure to entertain, sell ourselves and never appear to be visibly anxious keeps racking up.'[7] Such pressures remained the year that I started my career.

Even the self-help arena of that period was heavily geared towards combating shyness, being good at public speaking and appearing confident while networking. I remember devouring *Mrs Money-penny's Careers Advice for Ambitious Women*. Among other things, her advice includes gate-crashing events for networking opportunities. 'The trick I used was to turn up in an evening gown with an evening bag but no coat and then enter, looking as though I had just been outside for a cigarette.'[8] I never had the balls to go this far, but it was drilled into me (during my MA in publishing, my internship, from colleagues and indeed Moneypenny) that to get ahead, it was all about being good at networking, especially early in one's career. Which makes sense, if like me you have zero contacts in the area that you want to work in.

Everyone feels the pressure to fit a mould to some extent. At one point I even took a bloody course in it! Within mere minutes I knew

I lacked all of the attributes that the trainer was praising. 'Outgoing', 'gregarious', 'exuberant'. Nope, no and no again. 'You can learn to love networking!' He beamed. What he meant, in my opinion, was, 'You can learn to pretend to love networking.'

In other words, I was completely fucked (if I wanted to succeed that is). I'd have to try harder at developing my inner extroversion.

Fast-forward to the time of my breakdown and I'd spent a decade actively trying to change my personality and go against my instincts. Why was the panic happening? Because my brain had finally had enough. The stress of 'performing' all the time had become such a stressor that my amygdala associated it with danger. My subconscious rebelled.

It was an unexpected conclusion to reach. Up until this point I hadn't considered the idea that there was nothing wrong with the personality I was born with, or the dreams that I had.

What did I really want to do with my life? I wanted to be a writer. Even as I write that (how ironic), I cringe. *What kind of a nob wants to be a writer?* Also, *what kind of a self-indulgent nob spends time reflecting on what they want to do with their life?* Who did I think I was? Why couldn't I just be happy with whatever I was handed?

As with many things it was a lot simpler when I was a kid. I was consumed with reading and writing, and I very much intended to be a writer of some sort. Either that, or a historian, I hadn't decided. Unfortunately, neither profession was received with any level of enthusiasm from, well, anyone. Not that I expected to be coddled or overindulged. All creative industries are competitive; this is common knowledge. Hard work was mandatory, without any guarantee of success.

But I didn't expect to be shat on quite so much for voicing my aspirations!

Here's a tip: if you want to be a writer, don't bank on receiving encouraging, impartial advice from a failed writer, or from anyone not in a creative industry for that matter. I lost count of the number of times I was laughed at, patronised or straight up told that it wasn't going to happen in any capacity. Teachers, family, journalists who came into school to 'inspire' us.

Perhaps a stronger person might have stuck to their guns and ploughed ahead despite the backlash. I've always been in awe of people like this. Those who have a resolute and almost dogmatic self-belief that doesn't require encouragement. Rock star Courtney Love is a famous example of one such personality. I'm very aware that I lack the balls to be despised while 'chasing my dreams'. I value approval too much, or I did.

After a while, I just got fed up of disappointing people with my ambitions. Of seeing the look of confusion and then disapproval. It's more satisfying in the short term to please people. I admit that during this period I liked pleasing my parents far more than was healthy. Not just with good behaviour, but by making life choices that I knew they'd approve of. I had no real experience of the world after all and so I fed off their constant reassurance (another classic sign of anxiety).

I loved seeing their eyes light up with pride as they told extended family how well I was doing academically and what my plans were for the future. Like many millennials, I was the first in my family to go to university, let alone work in a creative industry. In many ways, pleasing others defined me, and I clung to that security.

In an interview with Elizabeth Day, bestselling author Jessie Burton relates to this, explaining that her success at school replaced her need to find her own identity. 'It was more or less a self-imposed state of doing things that garner applause or approval and therefore made me feel safe.'[9]

Like Jessie, I noticed that some things received approval (from family, teachers, friends, etc.) and others disdain. In order to be successful, I simply needed to stick to the things that everyone approved of. That way I wouldn't lose anything, or the love of anyone. As a teenager, I lived with a real fear that love was very much conditional and could be taken away if you said the wrong thing, or made the wrong choice. It's why I let so much slide. I thought love and approval were the same thing.

My ambitions, along with my genuine personality it turns out, were left outside in the cold. (I know, even I'm getting fucking bored of my self-pity now. But stay with me, it's all relevant!)

Looking back on my breakdown now, I recognise what my amygdala was trying to do. Despite causing so much chaos, I like to think that it was fighting to bring my true self back to the surface. It was protecting me from myself.

Starting the blog in 2013 really helped to calm this particular storm. Sure, there were a few crossed wires with my amygdala and the whole 'is this work, are you in DANGER?' But we got there. The blog was a passion project and allowed me to get back in touch with my creative spark. I finally stopped waiting to be given permission to write. As a kid, I'd write all the time because I wanted to, not because I wanted to achieve something. *Big Magic* by Elizabeth Gilbert is a cracking book that inspires creativity. You can be creative for creativity's sake, that is a valid goal. 'The sooner and more passionately you get married to this idea – that it is ultimately entirely up to you – the better off you'll be.'[10] If you want to write a zombie novel, then do it, or start portrait painting, or make your own wrapping paper. Your creative fun can remain private or become an active point of conversation. You don't need permission from a higher authority, just fucking do it for the sake of it. Oh, and btw there are other options than colouring books.

Along with wanting to help people, I started my blog to indulge this creative outlet and tell my story, and allowing me to be myself reduced the panic.

My generation

Statistics provided by Mental Health First Aid (MHFA) have detailed that one in four adults will experience at least one panic attack in their lifetime, one in ten will experience them frequently, and one in thirty will develop panic disorder. To put this into perspective, one in ten people have overstressed their fight-or-flight response so badly, that it can no longer recognise physical danger from emotional distress and exhaustion, thereby triggering regular panic attacks. That's fucked up. If you broke your leg, you wouldn't push yourself to run a marathon, yet the same respect is not afforded to the brain.

It's no secret that my generation, Generation Y, has been dealt a bad hand. Not only are there growing social and economic pressures – a lack of affordable housing, university debt, a failing jobs market – but there's also a growing unease because of major social changes (Brexit, coronavirus and the climate emergency) and what they might mean for our future.

The average age for first-time buyers has jumped from twenty-three in the 1960s to thirty in 2018. Research from Zoopla found that the standard deposit for a house in London, and other major cities is now £38,000. The rise in UK house prices has contributed to an increase in the numbers of young people renting property. In 2018, 55 per cent of those under the age of thirty-four were renting, compared to 35 per cent in 1998. Then there's the self-employment issue: unless you've been working for yourself consistently for two years, not a bank in the country will lend you a penny. I found this out the hard way. It doesn't matter how much you have in savings, or your projected earnings for the year. It's a no from the bank.

Journalist Niellah Arboine writes about the millennial mental health crisis for *Dazed & Confused*. 'According to the Mental Health Foundation in 2018, millennials are more stressed by work than any other generation. We're currently entering an era where being "booked and busy" is not only common but a sign of success and status.'[11] Based on my own experiences I'd have to agree with her. I felt at my most successful when I was swamped with work commitments.

Ellen Jones, award-winning speaker and campaigner, with a focus on LGBTQ+ rights, mental health and autism, gave me a great quote for this chapter. It's worth mentioning that in 2018 she won the first-ever MTV EMA Generation Change award in recognition of her campaigning. It's also worth mentioning that she's my amazing mate who's too clever for her own good! With regard to the pressures on Generation Y she had this to say: 'I think the biggest factor for me is actually the political climate which is incredibly volatile, and the effect that has on marginalised people, who are often the first to be vilified or ignored. The pace of life seems fairly relentless and there is a near constant expectation to be working, only there also aren't any jobs and the work exists only to survive, unless you are extremely rich. I think being aware of the issues going on in the world right now is an incredible gift in many ways but I would be lying if I said it doesn't send me into an existential spiral when I realise the planet is burning and people are dying because the rich are pursuing profit at the expense of everyone and everything.' Yup, that'll do it.

Add a nice dose of media pressure that 'we should have it all' before the age of thirty, and the expectation that you should display your perfect life on social media, and we have a recipe for a mental health crisis. 'Generation Y are NOT weak,' Dr Soph tells me passionately. 'The pressure is just so excruciating for millennials. They're the first generation to have everything that they do recorded and rated, from exams to social media. Society has created a pressure cooker.'

Emma Gannon, author of *The Multi-Hyphen Method*, refers to the 'Mac-owning Instagrammable #GirlBoss, running her business from a beach in Bali.'[12] I can completely relate to this notion that Generation Y feels great pressure to achieve success young. What with my two-year progression plan and desire to project the perfect life to others, I certainly felt the strain of my generation. In many ways, I feel like we were all stomping away blindly, praying that the tread-mill would stop, but not wanting to admit that we're struggling.

Is it really that surprising that so many of us burned out, without the proper tools to support ourselves? Even with all the recent cam-paigning, self-care is still very much promoted as a luxury, the last priority for all but a privileged few. Worse, it's become competitive on social media. On Instagram, as of May 2020, the hashtag #self-care has 27,770,096 posts. The majority of the feed is littered with images of people on a beach, or at a retreat, hands in the air looking wistfully away from the camera, as though they don't know they're being photographed. When did that become a thing, by the way? I like a nice photo as well as the next person, but come on now. The beautifully arranged 'clean' meals and juices, detoxes and yoga. Then there's the motivational quotes, a favourite of mine being: 'Self-care is a priority, not a luxury.' She says, as she sits looking at a sunset in Cannes.

Last-minute spa weekend? Sure, if you can blow £500. A yoga class at 6 a.m.? Not likely if you're a mum. Luxury silk sleep mask? Would any self-respecting individual spend £60 on this? No. That's why the only people who own them are influencers (who in most cases don't actually pay for this stuff). Speaking of which, despite what we see on Instagram, going to the Maldives for two weeks isn't exactly the standard of self-care that everyone can achieve. Apparently, self-care comes with a hefty price tag. A complicated response to something that should be as simple as running a bath and staying put for an hour.

Nadia James, the founder of Kinde, a mental health app, is keen to highlight this disparity. 'Self-care is an action you take, not a purchase you make. Those "treat yourself" moments are a small part of what self-care requires,' she says. 'In truth, we run the risk of excluding people who need self-care most when we focus on scented candles and yoga mats.' Hear hear, Nadia! Going round to my friend's house for a natter is the ultimate self-care for me.

Positive actions such as making time for yourself, eating well, or going to bed early have arguably been lost on my generation. Actual self-care has taken a back seat, which correlates with the rise of mental illness and panic attacks.

*

A few days after the *Evil Dead* epiphany, I found myself sitting down in a meeting room with several other colleagues. Within seconds I felt a wave of panic hit. However, on this occasion, rather than looking for an excuse to leave (toilet, water, etc.), I stayed put and thought to myself: *It's a trick. There's no danger here, the brain has been fooled, just like watching a horror film. Nothing bad will happen, it'll just be distressing and uncomfortable until it passes.*

Whenever I go into a meeting nowadays, I ask that the door be left open or, even better, if the organiser could open a window. I know that my brain associates fresh air with 'calm', therefore, an open window will keep my amygdala happy. At a recent meeting, a man objected about the window, complaining about the cold. Fair enough, it was the middle of winter. So, I handed him my coat and smiled, saying, 'Unless you want me to run around the room screaming, you'll keep it open.' It stayed open. Thank you, Tom!

Chapter 4

Panic on Stage: Public Speaking and Dealing with Your Inner Voice

Saturday 11th November 2017

The gorgeous woman standing directly in front of me has purple and pink hair. She's famous on one or more social media platforms, but for the life of me, I can't place her. Neither can my mum, but that's not quite as surprising. I'm in the green room at Stylist Live, a very cool event that includes fashion, art, and inspirational talks on subject matters central to women. In twenty minutes' time, I'll be making a speech. So, it's hardly surprising that my mind is elsewhere. In 'hell' to be precise.

Why have I agreed to do this? Why, of all people, did they ask me?

Since the publication of my first book *We're All Mad Here*, I've been approached regularly to deliver talks at various events. Someone with social anxiety engaging in public speaking? The irony isn't lost on me. Yet, the fact I'm asked back is testament, I suppose, to the techniques I've learned. I live with panic, but I refuse to let it control my life any more than, say, a heavy period. You know the type. Big knickers, feeling like your uterus is being crushed in a vice, bloated, brain fog, fatigue and crying because you put your slippers on the wrong feet. Still, we manage it with as much dignity as possible.

'What's your following like?' Pink-purple hair girl asks, smiling warmly.

'It's me, her dad, her husband and a few friends,' my mum answers, beaming back at her.

'She means on social media, Mum,' I explain.

'Oh well in that case, hundreds. At least two hundred I'd say.'

It's a lot more than that, but I don't correct her. It's a slippery slope, the old 'follower count,' and I prefer to torture myself in other ways. Like humiliating myself in front of a lecture hall full of people, for example. *What the fuck are you doing here? This is really bad. Although, pause the freak out for a moment because you just clocked a load of free Fiji water in the corner. Stick a few bottles in Mum's bag before you forget.*

A woman with a clipboard and a walkie-talkie bursts into the room and shouts, 'Claire Eastham!' My stomach drops in response and I have the urge to shit myself for the sixth time this afternoon. For a moment, I consider hiding behind the lurid green sofa to my left, but my mum is already waving proudly, and the woman approaches us. 'This is your ten-minute call. We're going to take you to get mic'd up.' She doesn't wait for a response and darts off into the hallway. Mum and I follow like schoolchildren, scurrying and stumbling after her. My legs feel like jelly as I descend the stairs, and the sense of dread is overwhelming. *You can't do this. You just can't. But you don't want to let everyone down. Your family and friends have come all this way to see you.* I mean, it's London, not Dubai, but whatever.

The woman stops abruptly, causing me to bump into her. 'Look over there!' She's pointing to a large queue behind us. 'That's all the people who are waiting to hear you talk.' *Fuck.* I don't have much time to gawk, as she's hotfooting it away again. *This is going to be far worse than your breakdown, what if you can't handle it? You're going to humiliate yourself in front of hundreds of people, except this time they'll be no recovering. Your career as an author will be over. This is the end. You need to cancel it while you still can.*

Triggers

The first therapist that I ever saw asked me to identify my triggers. 'What triggered your first panic attack?' The question initially frustrated me, because the answer was obviously, 'an interview', which I'd already told her about. However, I'd experienced interviews before and not reacted this way. So what was different about that particular interview? My discoveries in chapters 2 and 3 proved that it was a build-up of stress over a five-year period.

I worry that the word 'trigger' has become negatively associated with the 'snowflake' generation. Yet another name for us millennials. A snowflake, according to a certain section of the online community, is someone who is too fragile and sensitive for this world, who is too weak to handle offensive content in literature and films, and demands that 'trigger warnings' be used. Although, to be honest, I wouldn't mind a warning before delving unknowingly into a text that covers slavery, torture, rape or any other form of abuse.

A trigger is something that sets off a memory flashback, transporting the person back to the event of his/her original trauma. It can be activated by any of the five senses: sight, sound, touch, smell and taste. Once triggered, the person will react to this flashback with an emotional intensity similar to that at the time of the trauma.

A personal example of this would be the 'Braveheart incident'. I was eight years old and Dad was watching *Braveheart* on TV. I walked into the room at the wrong moment and caught the scene in which William Wallace's wife gets her throat cut. As I watched the blade slice across her vocal cords I was overwhelmed with horror. I screamed and grabbed my own throat in response. I swear I could feel the blade; even now, as I write this I can still feel it. What followed next was an hour of tears, shouting and me being put to bed early with a Disney film playing in the background. (This is still my go-to tactic to alleviate trauma.)

I thought about *that* scene every day for a month. I still don't like people touching my neck, as Dan found out when he playfully tried to tickle me. After laughing initially, I flipped out, pushing him away hard, 'I don't like that!' I screamed, my heart pounding and my face flushed. I didn't realise until then that even after twenty years it still had such a hold on me. Of course, the odds of me being tied to a post and executed were slim. It wasn't rational and I certainly wasn't in any danger, yet my brain reacted.

A classic example of trauma was experienced by soldiers in the First World War and was called 'shell shock' before it was officially renamed as post-traumatic stress disorder (PTSD).

After being stationed in the trenches for extended periods, in which bombardment from shell fire was common, the strain began to take its toll on the psyche of the men. In many cases, after an initial bout of mania, the trauma lay dormant, the memories shut out by the brain as a form of protection. A patient could find himself walking down the street to be triggered by the sound of a car backfiring or a shop door being slammed shut. What followed was hysteria and panic as the man dived to the floor, or ran out of the shop yelling, feeling threatened but not understanding why.

> I wondered what was happening because anything that went off, bang, over there somewhere, made me jump. And I suddenly realised I'd got this thing called shell shock, which I'd never believed in before.
> – **British officer F. Jourdain**

Robert Graves's famous memoir *Goodbye to All That*, first published in 1929, depicts his service in the First World War, and he writes about the soldiers who were damaged psychologically by the trenches. 'The unfortunate ones were officers who had endured two years or more of continuous trench service. In many cases they became dipsomaniacs. I knew three or four who had worked up to the point of two bottles of whiskey a day.'[1] Alcohol abuse was a common coping technique for trauma. It still is, along with other things.

However, despite its historical connection to warfare, PTSD is not solely experienced by soldiers. According to mental health research charity MQ, over two million people in the UK live with the condition, which can be caused by anything from military service to a traumatic childbirth. It's a type of anxiety disorder triggered by traumatic events in a person's life such as real or threatened death, severe injury or sexual assault. It was first studied between 1878 and 1893 by French neurologist Jean-Martin Charcot, who published over twenty case studies that detail what he called 'traumatic hysteria'.[2]

People with PTSD usually experience nightmares, flashbacks, and vivid upsetting memories of what they went through. They may also feel very anxious and 'on edge', and may try to avoid being reminded of the traumatic event.

Perhaps controversially, I've always likened a panic attack to a genuine traumatic event. While not in any physical harm, the brain is unable to recognise this during the attack and it therefore reacts in the same way that it would if physical danger was a reality. Basically, if you truly believe that you're about to die, it doesn't matter about the truth of the situation, your brain thinks, *FUCK I'M GOING TO DIE* and then afterwards, *FUCK, I NEARLY DIED.*

Is a near-death experience any different if the brain can't categorise the difference? Panic may be a trick, but it doesn't make the experience any less real to the person experiencing it. This theory also applies to triggers and what can prompt future attacks.

On many occasions, I haven't realised that my brain has even clocked a trigger until I'm in the eye of the storm, so to speak. The amygdala is a sensory sponge and the smallest thing can set it off. Perhaps it spots an especially large table and likens it to an office meeting room. DANGER. Or I unexpectedly find myself the centre of attention. DANGER. Next thing I know, the wave hits and I feel the attack crash over me.

Public speaking is something that makes the majority of people feel nervous, no matter how experienced they are. It's also recognised as a top – if not the top – phobia (glossophobia) that can trigger panic.

The most common panic attack triggers include:

- Public speaking
- Flying
- Eating in public

- Driving
- Work
- Social events
- Supermarkets
- Health concerns

Interestingly, all of the above relate to situations/environments in which we have limited control.

For me, any environment that reminded me of work was a potential trigger, and wasn't limited to being in the office itself.

For others, a trigger can be a physical change or a reaction to fatigue. In the summer of 2019, I met Nadiya Hussain, winner of *The Great British Bake Off* in 2015. At the time, she was filming a documentary about anxiety and panic, both of which she has herself. After the filming was complete, we had lunch and bonded over our love for stodgy northern food. At the time, Nadiya was at the beginning of her journey towards understanding her panic attacks and I was inspired by her honesty. Not many people can be as open with a stranger, in my experience. At one point. she asked me whether there's a cure. Had I found a magic wand, so to speak? 'If I'd found it do you really think I'd give it to you!' She laughed delightedly at my cheeky response, popping antacids like sweets. (The life of a foodie!)

She later agreed to open up more about her experiences and I asked her about triggers. 'I want to say that I know what my triggers are, but they are so hit-and-miss sometimes. I know that when I am tired and overworked, I often feel it rising. It's usually a build-up for me.'

Her response isn't uncommon. Others I've spoken to claim that tiredness or feeling run-down makes them more susceptible to panic. I'm definitely more sensitive if I haven't slept well.

Other people's emotions can be triggering for me too. Before I went on *The Jo Good Show*, my mum was with me in the waiting area. 'Oh God, I'm nervous, I don't know how you do it, Claire!' she said.

'What do you mean *you're* nervous? I'm the one in the sodding firing line!'

The interview went well, but I was wired for hours afterwards.

Emotional contagion is the aptly named term for 'catching' other people's emotions. Are you a sympathetic crier? Do you find laughing infectious? Well, I catch nerves as easily as catching a cold. It's a really shit superpower that also applies to anger, boredom and anxiety, but nerves are the front-runner. I can't cope if I think that people are scared on my behalf. It makes the pressure *not* to have a panic attack for their sake overwhelming.

By the time Stylist Live came along, Mum had learned how to keep a poker face. I needed her to be upbeat and confident, even if she was internally bricking it.

After every attack that I have, I like to analyse what happened in the moments before the attack to make me feel unsafe. Was it the click of the office door closing? Or the high temperature? Was it because I hadn't slept well the night before? There's a lot of drilling down when it comes to panic. I like to think of it as an ongoing investigation.

Once I worked out what my main triggers were, I could take steps to help myself. For example, I rarely meet my agent in his office. We go to a cafe instead. I'm also happy to ask family members not to accompany me to public-speaking events. People tend to be understanding if you're open with them. This is not to be confused with 'avoidance', by the way, whereby a person deliberately avoids a situation where they've had a panic attack previously. My biggest trigger,

I've found, is the use of my name. What the fuck is that all about? It could probably be linked back to school. In my mind, the use of my name equals 'you've done something bad' or 'you're about to be made to do something unpleasant'.

Trash talk

For as long as I can remember I've had an inner critic, like a lot of people. An unconscious monologue that circulates around my mind unchecked. He isn't the nicest of characters, but that's just him. (No, he doesn't have a name, but it's definitely a male voice that I hear. Loud and cutting.) I began to notice him more as I entered my teens and this can probably be linked to me going through puberty. My friend Natasha Devon also deals with a male entity, who she calls 'Nigel,' a lump in her throat that flares up when she's having a bad day. But my voice remains nameless, the closest I've come to a label is 'him'. He points out my mistakes, reminds me that I'll never be good enough, what a horrible person I am and lets me know what other people think about me. Spoiler alert: it's always bad. *You're thick, do you know that? You've always been a waste of space, Claire. People will think you're weak, you can't cope with anything.*

Nothing unusual here, this is textbook anxiety and my therapist at the time helped me to understand that these intrusive thoughts were a symptom of the condition.

Along with boxing, Muhammad Ali was famous for what became known as 'trash talk'. A stream of verbal abuse that sticks. 'Ain't Liston ugly? He's too ugly to be world champion. The world champ should be pretty, like me.' I began to call my inner voice trash talk. It helped to identify when it was happening.

What's the use of trash talk?

During and before a panic attack, my inner voice becomes louder, more insistent and finally unbearable. Have you ever tried to argue with yourself? It doesn't work. No matter how many times you try and reason with the brain – *it's fine, we're not in danger* – it turns into a broken record, repeating the same fears. As David Carbonell says, you will never win an argument with your amygdala because its sole purpose is to identify danger and keep you alive. 'This is why people notice "the harder I try, the worse it gets". They're putting out fires with gasoline.'

From my investigation of the symptoms, I know that each symptom of panic has a recognisable use in the survival stakes However, it wasn't until I started doing public speaking that I realised 'trash talk' was also a symptom of panic. Its purpose is the same as all the other symptoms: to keep me safe.

The talk may take on different approaches, for example, insulting: *You'll humiliate yourself if you stay, leave now!* Or hysterical: *You can't breathe, you're going to die!* Or in some cases unhinged and ridiculous: *What if the ceiling collapses and buries us all alive?* It's overwhelming, drowning out all other noise. But as intrusive and insulting as it is, trash talk is all about ensuring that I stay alive. It has a purpose, even though it feels random and chaotic.

From past experiences, here is a list of the most common 'trash talk' panic has thrown at me:

- I'm going to vomit/piss myself/sweat all over the floor
- I'm going to look stupid in front of X

- I can't do this
- I can't cope
- Everybody will think I'm crazy
- My heart will explode
- I'll suffocate
- I'll act bizarrely (e.g., strip naked in a meeting and start screaming)
- I'll hurt someone

It took me a long time to realise that all of these statements essentially mean the same thing, and that is: I FEEL AFRAID. I didn't want to accept this initially – surely my fears were more sophisticated than that. 'Most panic trash starts with "what if", and "what if" equals "I'm scared",' Carbonell informs me. Cracking this code gave me a sense of peace. Panic is not a fortune-teller, a premonition of our end, or a sign that something bad is certain to happen. In basic terms it just means 'I'm scared.' Remember the David Guetta song 'Titanium'? Think of the lyrics. A panic attack trash talk is *exactly* this. The amygdala steals attention with noise and drama, but it isn't a certainty of danger to come.

As with many of my encounters with panic symptoms, I learned how to deal with trash talk purely by accident. I was on the bus early one morning and this kid in front of me was behaving like a demon, to put it lightly. Screaming, crying, throwing stuff, the usual tantrum shit. He demanded attention with every single action, and nothing that his poor mother tried would soothe him. I envy that, by the way, the freedom toddlers have to express their emotions so openly, without fear of judgement. Eventually she sighed and announced: 'OK, well I don't know what you want, Jack, so you can just fuss if you want to.' The kid was so shocked that he stopped shrieking. By accepting the tantrum and choosing not to react, the mother had extinguished the kid's power. *Fuck me, that's some powerful psychology.* By the way, I'm not a parent, so I have no idea if this was a good course of action. But whatever, it worked, and the kid sat quietly, tantrum forgotten. Mums really are bloody impressive!

At the time, I was on my way to a meeting with an editor and I was nervous. *What if you have a panic attack?* my brain hissed. *They'll think you're unhinged and you won't get the gig.* I was about to argue back, when it hit me: trash talk is like the screaming kid. You can't win by arguing or trying to appease it, you just have to let it scream. In his book, *Understanding Panic Attacks and Overcoming Fear*, Roger Baker writes: 'People who are afraid of (intrusive) thoughts often try and push them from their mind. The effort involved in doing this means that they are spending a lot of time concentrating on the thoughts, making them more likely to intrude.'[3] Basically, it's like a snake eating its own tail. In order to break the cycle, I needed to change my behaviour.

Tom, an animator and follower of my blog had the same realisation:

I was just so tired of fighting. There's only so much rationalising you can do. It felt like my brain was a nagging spouse who I never agreed to marry in the first place! All I ever heard was that 'I'd die if I went out tonight,' or that 'I shouldn't talk to X person because I'll look like a dick.' In the end I just gave in. I had no idea that that was the key! Who would've thought that not fighting was the best way to fight? The nagging wife is still there, but I don't take her on any more.

Claire Weekes wrote about 'masterly inactivity' with regard to panic attacks: 'to stop holding tensely on to yourself, trying to control your fear, trying "to do something about it" while subjecting yourself to constant self-analysis'.[4] I came to understand that accepting fear makes it dissipate. The way to regain a sense of calm is to go along with the sensations of panic, rather than oppose them. This goes against all of my instincts and the idea of not trying to 'fix' the problem was obscene. I was used to writing all my worries down and rationalising them in various CBT exercises that helped with social anxiety. Still, they clearly didn't help with panic and I was willing to try anything. Masterly inactivity is a tough sell, but she's right. The easiest way to take control back from panic and from trash talk was to relinquish it.

So, I did just that. I let the trash talk flow, listing all the horrible things that could go wrong, or ways that I might embarrass myself, and I didn't react other than to think: *OK, cheers for that.* I might not be able to control the thoughts that pop into my head, but I can decide whether or not to take action and this is comforting.

The five minutes before my talk begins are some of the longest of my life. My entire body is slick with sweat and I can barely feel my feet on the ground. It's as though I've floated out of my body and am paralysed from shock. The trash talk goes up a gear.

Cancel NOW. You can still cancel, just tell them that you don't feel well. This is a huge mistake. Everyone in this room is about to witness your humiliation. Just cancel now and we can get out of here. There's no shame in it, nobody will judge you.

I don't respond, I just sit there silently and let the moments pass one agonising second at a time.

I don't know how I get on to the stage, but I obviously have because I'm now standing behind the podium with my PowerPoint presentation projecting behind me and a bright light illuminating my face. My heart pounds and adrenaline circulates through my veins like a storm. *You stupid bitch, what have you done?*

I take a deep breath from my stomach and let the sensation wash over me once more, along with the trash talk. *I'm afraid. It's OK to be afraid,* I say to myself calmly. *Thank you for your concern, but I've checked and nothing bad is going to happen. In fact, the worse that I'm going to feel is right this second; it can only get better from here. So, fuck it. Even if I fall on my face, it's cool. I'll just get back up.*

The abuse continues, but I accept it and don't react. Then I take things a step further. I do something that I haven't planned and have *never* done before. I scan the room, take another breath and speak clearly into the microphone: 'My name is Claire Eastham and I'd like to admit to you all now, that I'm afraid. I live with social anxiety disorder and public speaking makes me nervous. Can I get a round of applause for that?'

As the room explodes with applause, I know for certain that every-thing is going to be OK … and my inner voice is silent for the rest of the talk. I am still out of my comfort zone, but I don't feel crippled by the fear any more. In fact, after five minutes I start to enjoy myself.

I don't love public speaking and the thought of it still makes me uncomfortable, but I can do it without too much distress these days. The key is in the prep: understanding my triggers, anticipating what the trash talk might say and working out how I can get through the experience as comfortably as possible.

CHAPTER 5

Panic at Work and Laughter, the Superpower

'There is an unspoken message hidden within a chuckle, that says I promise, you'll get through this.'
– Art Buchwald, Pulitzer Prize-winning journalist

'I know this sounds crazy, but I'm worried I might take my top off and run around the room screaming.'

I blurt this out to Wendy, the sixty-year-old head of catering for the company I was working for at the time. I'd arrived early for a scheduled meeting, fifteen minutes to be precise. The idea was to 'take in the room' and prepare myself, but in fact, it just made me more on edge. I was already having a bad day mentally, my anxiety scoring points at every opportunity. I'd been back at work for nine weeks and this was my first proper meeting since the 'incident'. A sales meeting, if I remember correctly, the type that happens monthly. Ten or so people attend and at least 50 per cent of the agenda is white noise.

What if you run out again? They'll be no coming back this time. You'll lose your job. (Intrusive thoughts tend to be repetitive, by the way. This can be a good thing. It makes them easier to identify.)

I pictured the look on my colleagues' faces in this nightmare fantasy, confused and embarrassed on my behalf. Is there anything worse than people being embarrassed on your behalf?

The approaching storm was evident from the familiar sense of dread I felt deep in my gut as I tried in vain to take a deep breath. The tingling in my limbs had set in and my heart was pounding so loud I wondered if Wendy could hear it over the mini Hoover she was operating. I was scared and desperate. *How the fuck am I going to get out of this?* I couldn't exactly pull another Jane Austen stunt. Or could I? *Perhaps I could excuse myself, go to the toilets and just not come back? There'd be questions though and confusion that leads to more questions.* I took another deep breath, to no avail. *Or maybe I could pretend that a family member had been rushed into hospital? Although, knowing these lot they'd probably be really nice and considerate about it and rearrange the meeting to suit me. Bastards.* Seven minutes to go; I was running out of time.

Unaware of my internal meltdown, Wendy placed coffee cups on the boardroom table and carefully arranged the biscuits. I glared at her incredulously, waiting for her to notice. *How can I be in pit of fire on one side of the room and yet Wendy carries on as normal?*

She was battling a smudge with a cloth and some polish when I continued. 'I feel like I'm going to freak out and scream! Like proper scream, like "there's a man with an axe heading straight for us!" scream,' I blurt out, close to tears.

Continuing to polish (fingerprint stains being the bane of her life), she sighed and without looking up replied, 'Well if you do, I might join you, love. It'd certainly liven things up around here!'

I stared at her, confused, stunned even, but to this day, I still want to kiss her for such a genius response. After a pause, we both burst out laughing. Loud, screeching, belly-laughing, and it felt good. It was so unexpected and cut through the storm.

I'd always known Wendy to be one of those incredible people in life who don't ask questions and who don't judge, no matter what. Whether you were hungover on Monday morning, having an affair with your PA, or threatening to strip off in a meeting, you could confess all to Wendy and she'd take it in her stride. 'If you're going to take your top off then you might as well jump on the table too.' She had a point. Go big or go home. Panic had made me believe that I was about to lose control, but the spectacle that it had chosen to taunt me with now seemed comical (as in, me running around the room in my bra while Mike the sales director tried to deliver the latest regional data). As I laughed, I realised that the room had stopped spinning and I didn't feel quite so consumed by terror. Was this even possible? Had humour dissolved panic in some way?

I tested the theory once more. 'Have you done much table-dancing in your time, Wendy?'

She shook her head. 'Not since I turned sixty, love, my tits aren't what they used to be.'

We laughed some more, and for the first time all morning, I felt grounded, as though I'd found my way back to earth.

Research conducted by Adzooma showed that on average, people will spend 90,000 hours at work before retirement, which is a third of their lives.[1] Yet, the workplace is listed as one of the biggest triggers of mental discord. Heavy workloads, long hours, office politics, difficult clients, insufficient breaks and the pressure to succeed all lead to high levels of continuous stress to the amygdala. The different pressures brought by work can make us feel 'under threat'. Dr Paul MacLean sums it up as follows: 'the world changed faster than the brain could evolve'.[2] Prehistoric dwellers were threatened by tigers; modern man is threated by deadlines and micromanaging.

None of this information is anything new; we've been hearing about the culture of 'overworking' in self-help books and wellness articles for years. It's become a key feature of modern culture, a satire almost, which despite being aware of we struggle to change. 'Don't work yourself into the ground,' a teacher friend of mine messages, as she marks homework at 10 p.m.!

The coronavirus pandemic in 2020 unexpectedly highlighted this further with the enforced lockdown. Hosts of people have reported that their mental health has improved as a result of being away from work. An article in the *Guardian* featured an interview with a variety of people, including a university lecturer living with generalised anxiety disorder: 'Since the pace of life slowed due to the pandemic and he stopped commuting, he has experienced a sense of profound relief, more energy, and an improvement in his anxiety. "My usual life feels like a pinball machine. You're whacking the buttons and the paddles are flailing around, sometimes not even making contact, and it just doesn't feel like that any more."'[3]

After years of abusing my amygdala, work became my biggest threat, but I felt powerless to do anything about it. It's not as though I could 'opt out', like a community bake sale. When I came back after a month-long absence (I wanted to do two weeks, fortunately the doctor insisted on four), I was worried about how this might impact my career. It wasn't an incident that I could merely brush off, like having 'one too many' at the work Christmas do and falling into a bush (which incidentally I have also done). Ninety days prior, I ran out of a meeting room babbling like a coked-up Elizabeth Bennet in *Pride and Prejudice*, so there was no hiding that something was wrong. Anxiety and panic were on the official doctor's note, and from the way people were walking on eggshells around me, there was no denying that word had spread. 'Claire has a mental health condition, so be extra nice.' Not that moving up the career ladder was high on my agenda during that period; I was traumatised enough by what had happened to take my recovery seriously, in the same way that a professional footballer with a broken ankle would respect the recovery process, despite their desire to continue.

Still, I couldn't help but feel a twitch of concern for the future. Would people worry that I couldn't cope? Would I be trusted with anything important again?

There's been a lot of progression in the last five years with regard to mental health rights and education. Simon Blake, CEO of Mental Health First Aid, claims: 'Mental health is now recognised legally in the workplace. We want everyone to know that they have rights that employers will recognise.' The Equality Act 2010 protects disabled people from unfair treatment, and this includes people with a mental illness. In other words, a person cannot be sacked simply for having depression, anxiety or another mental illness. Thanks to organisations such as MHFA, major corporations are starting to invest more in mental health education.

Campaigner Natasha Devon took things a step further and founded the Where's Your Head At? campaign. After over a decade of delivering talks in schools about mental health and body image, she decided to target the over-thirties, who had not grown up with access to mental health education. I asked her about the campaign in more detail.

'I realised that I needed to target workplaces. Around the same time, I met up with Lucie Cave, who is Editorial Director of Bauer Media, looking after brands such as *Grazia* magazine and KISS FM. Lucie said Bauer were keen to do something really impactful around mental health and together we cooked up a campaign to make mental health first aid mandatory in all medium to large workplaces, in the same way regular (or physical) first aid is. Lucie somehow managed to get every single Bauer brand to conduct their own mini-campaign, led by voices who would resonate with their respective audiences (I cannot emphasise enough how much of an impressive feat this was). Meanwhile, I designed a survey to be sent out across all Bauer brands to get a flavour of where the public were with their mental health, started a change.org petition and brought in Mental Health First Aid England as co-directors of the campaign, who provide the gold standard of mental health training in this country. As expected, the Bauer survey showed that it was challenges in and surrounding the workplace that were cited as the biggest negative influence on British people's mental health, with 1 in 6 people having experienced a mental health issue (such as a panic attack) while at work.'

She personally delivered a petition with more than 200,000 signatures to the prime minister and the campaign gained widespread support. The proposed law change was being debated in Parliament but has yet to be passed.

I can't complain about my back-to-work experience. I was treated very well, the publisher I worked for at the time was ahead of the game when it came to mental health awareness and I felt supported.

However, in the larger scale of the company, I couldn't help but feel as though I'd just derailed my career. They wouldn't sack me, that much was certain, but would there forever be a black mark next to my name? Could I trust upper management not to be biased towards me in future? This is a concern that I hear time and again after delivering workplace talks. The job titles may vary, but at every level there exists a fear of stigma that prevents panic sufferers from opening up to colleagues and getting the support they need. 'I can't let anyone else know that I have panic attacks. They won't say anything to my face, but I know I'll be penalised for it,' Kate, a trainee coder from Manchester, tells me.

'There's a difference between having an honest conversation about how panic affects me and what my employer can offer support-wise … And then there's being sat opposite a HR person who is merely ticking a box. They can't sack me, but it doesn't mean that they fully understand.' As Kate later found out when her manager noticed that she'd been crying: 'You're not going to have time off are you?' she spat. 'We have several projects to complete by Friday.' Kate was indeed hoping to have a few days off to recover and visit her GP. 'After what she said, I knew that I daren't. She had the power to promote me, after all. I had to stay in her good books. So, I white-knuckled it, stayed late each night and neglected to prioritise my health. Then spent the entire weekend in bed trying to recover.'

I can appreciate her concerns because they were mine four years ago. Is the employment system biased against people who have panic attacks? Or indeed, any form of mental health condition?

I talked to Ruth Cooper-Dickson, founder of Champs, a global consultancy that provides mental health and wellbeing training. Ruth has worked with some of the largest corporations in the UK and around the world.

'We all have biases, it is part of human nature and we cannot understand everyone's frame of reference. Not everyone has experienced mental illness or dealt with someone who is struggling, or they may have had a particular experience which has shaped how they feel about mental ill health. Trust is always hard to build with any human and with your manager knowing, if you are open this will not go against you.'

This may be a harsh and sobering point, but she's right. There are no guarantees that a person won't be judged for any aspect of their identity, let alone being open about a mental illness. Women are still less likely to be offered a job over a man due to the 'threat of future maternity leave'. Not to mention, as Emma Gannon highlights: 'a woman is still paid 22 per cent less per hour than a man. It is assumed that they value work relationships more than money.'[4]

Despite various educational and awareness campaigns, I'm sceptical about their long-term impact. As a great cynic, I'd be off-brand if I weren't. Sure, people attend the mental health talk organised by HR and they try the free mindfulness class at lunchtime, but does it really alter attitudes long term?

Personally, I think it takes generations for prejudice to be phased out. Stigma is maintained by a lack of understanding and understanding often comes from personal experience. A boss who has never experienced depression might not understand why a colleague can't get out of bed, let alone come to work. Said colleague might be labelled as 'weak' or 'lazy', when in fact they're very ill. Whereas, a cold or a bad case of the shits has been experienced by most people, making it easier to sympathise.

Before the breakdown, colleagues could never understand why I got 'so worked up' about speaking in meetings or networking events.

'Nobody is focusing on you,' was a favourite statement batted around, as though this would immediately drive out the crazy from my brain. It's natural that people respond to irrational behaviour with rationality, but it rarely helps a person living with anxiety. How could I explain this or expect them to understand? *The thing is, Anna, my whole body seizes up and I can barely remember my name, let alone be glib. There's a constant stream of abuse circulating through my brain and I spend most social interactions analysing people's faces and body language, trying to assess whether or not they hate me. Vodka? Sounds great.*

Bias and prejudice in the workplace are nothing new, and not limited to mental illness. It felt like too big a beast to confront.

At the time I had to assess what was more of a priority, my recovery and feeling supported in my current job, or worrying about future problems that I couldn't control and may never occur. So I let that one go.

Did I progress within the company over the remaining two years I was there? Sadly not. Still, I like to think that was my decision. I was ready to move on and test out a new environment. It felt like a proactive step.

I wasn't going to ignore my condition in any area of my life going forward; it would be foolish as I'd come so far in recovery. This is not to say that the idea of 'coming out' to a new employer didn't fill me with dread, but all that would come in time. (Naturally after the three-month probation period!)

This promise to my brain was tested almost immediately in my second job, at a small, independent and rather eccentric publisher. A mere three days into the role I was informed that I'd be giving a presentation the following week to around thirty people. No joke. I would present twelve of our upcoming books to an external team who'd be selling them all over the world. Normally this would be done by the editor, but seeing as he was on holiday, I was expected to step in. 'That's not a problem is it?' he asked pleasantly. 'Not at all!' I smile. What else could I say? *Actually no, the thing is, the thought of giving a presentation in front of my own reflection, let alone thirty professionals, makes me wish I was dead. I was hoping to drop this bomb well after my probation meeting when you couldn't bin me without pay.*

Despite a bumpy start, the whole thing went surprisingly well. For starters, the 85-year-old CEO was even more batshit than me and not only answered his phone in the first two minutes of the presentation: 'Hello? HELLO! I can't talk right now, Bob, I'm stuck in a dark room full of strangers!' (Imagine the whole thing said in a strong New York accent.) After which he promptly fell asleep and was snoring so loudly it was hard for even the most serious audience members not to laugh. Turns out that this bizarre exchange was the perfect icebreaker! It rerouted my brain and although I was still experiencing panic, it no longer felt overwhelming. The humour liberated me. Oh, and, Bob, if you're reading this, cheers for the call!

The power of humour

At his public execution, prolific murderer William Palmer is said to have looked at the trapdoor on the gallows and asked the hangman, 'Are you sure it's safe?'

Black comedy has long been a sort of an obsession of mine, the more inappropriate the better. It's a powerful thought, the idea that laughter can remove you from a bleak situation, if only temporarily.

A therapist once commented that I use it as a diversion tactic and that I'd transform into 'comedy Claire' whenever she asked a question that made me uncomfortable.

Therapist: How are you sleeping at the moment?
Me: In a bed mainly, but I have been known to pass out on the couch.

Yet up until this point, I hadn't considered it a tool for panic.

Humour as therapy is very popular with the positive psychology movement).

According to credited academic researcher Barbara Crăciun, humour can have both physical and mental benefits.

'Laughing elevates the pain threshold and can help break the cycle between pain, sleep loss, depression, and immunosuppression. It lowers blood pressure, epinephrine, and glucose levels, and increases glucose tolerance. Laughter also assists in the recovery and prevention of cancer by increasing natural killer cell activity, the response of gamma interferon and T cells, and improves the defence against respiratory infections. Laughter produces a discharge of endorphins with both euphoric and calming effects.'[5]

In that meeting room with Wendy, laughter had allowed me to put some distance between myself and fear. Was that a deliberate move by my brain? Or was it a coincidence?

I thought back to the year before I moved to London, when my hamster Ronnie was dying and I stayed up half the night in hysterics. In the vet's waiting room my heart was pounding and my mouth was dry. I was probably having a low-level panic attack now that I think about it. As the vet confirmed that yes Ronnie was indeed dying, I burst into tears, convinced that I would never stop.

'Does he live on his own?' the vet asked.

'What?'

'The hamster, does he live on his own?'

'NO! He lives with me!' I blubbered.

'No ... I mean, do any other hamsters live in his cage with him?'

In my fragile state I thought he was asking whether Ronnie had a studio apartment down the road. My sobs were immediately swallowed by laughter, and the fear that had gripped me so intensely in the waiting room loosened its grasp.

(Ronnie did die three days later though. I buried him in a Molton Brown box.)

Humour is an adverse reaction to stress, providing both the brain and body with comfort. Or as Freud noted: 'A coping technique. By seeing the funny side, the individual can evaluate the situation as being less threatening and so responding with a lower level of the sympathetic nervous system. The decrease can therefore eventually lead to relaxation.'

Laughing enabled me to detach myself from uncomfortable thoughts and emotions. A result that up until this point had only been achieved by alcohol.

Yet how far could we go with this? Is laughter a form of therapy? Could it be deployed tactically to ease a panic attack?

An opportunity to trial this arose on my wedding day. Panic struck as I was having my hair done. The thought of walking down the aisle with all eyes on me suddenly felt suffocating. *What if you trip? Or worse, what if you vomit all over your dress. How will you continue with the day after something as humiliating as that?* I leant forward and asked for a moment to gather myself. I wanted to enjoy my wedding day, not endure it, and the idea that panic would somehow dominate things filled me with despair. *Not today. PLEASE. Not today.* I begged.

Fortunately, my legend of a friend Bec acted quickly. 'Claire, look!' she shouted. I looked up and she flashed me her tits, then proceeded to dance obscenely while singing: 'Whey hey heeeeeeeeey!' The hairdresser was naturally confused but polite enough not to comment. Bec's action did the trick and I cracked up laughing.

Laughter allowed me to take ownership of my fear, rather than feeling enslaved to it. It put some much needed distance between myself and panic.

I talked to my friend Aaron Gillies, author of *How to Survive the End of the World*, about this. As a fellow panic attack voyager, he understands the grip of fear better than most. He values humour as being one of the most effective tools. 'I use it in all of my writings around mental health. If I can make fun of it, I can make it feel smaller than it is, make it feel like you control it, instead of it controlling you.'

'If you can't joke about the most horrendous things in the world, what's the point of jokes? What's the point in having humour? Humour is to get us over terrible things.'

– **Ricky Gervais**

Laughter yoga

I first heard about laughter yoga from a random article online and didn't take it too seriously. When you've been in the wellbeing game for as long as I have you become almost jaded. It was most likely a fad, and visions of people giggling while in the downward dog position danced through my head.

Yet, as part of the research for this chapter, I decided to take a closer look and was surprised by what I found. Not only is laughter yoga recognised and legitimate, it's also very popular!

Pioneered in the 1960s and made famous by physician Dr Madan Kataria in 1995, laughter yoga encourages participants to mimic or fake the act of laughing, with the goal of achieving positive psychological outcomes.

Great, but what psychological outcomes exactly? Maybe this is why several weeks later, I found myself taking part in a laughter yoga class via Zoom, with laughter yoga expert Lotte Mikkelsen and the man Dr K himself.

I'd spoken to Lotte before the class and her enthusiasm for laughter yoga is infectious.

A random fact about me before we continue. I can't cry . . . That's not true exactly, I mean I have cried over the years, but this changed when I started taking sertraline, a side effect of which makes crying difficult. This is not to say that I don't feel sad, I just can't fucking cry! (Think Cameron Diaz's character in the film, *The Holiday*.)

Straight away Lotte points out that my issue with crying is probably why I'm drawn to laughter as a therapeutic tool. 'Laughing and crying are not opposites, they're a continuum,' she explains. 'They flow from the same place and release tension in the body. Think of them as healing and cleansing.'

An acupuncturist said something similar to me during an appointment: 'Crying is a necessary cleanse for the brain,' but then she also talked a lot about poo, which was far less enchanting.

Lotte enquires whether I experience tremors (yes) and is quick to point out that this is another way that the body releases tension. 'Cortisol and adrenaline have to exit the body and the brain will find a way to achieve this.' Unfortunately, shaking and crying tend to make others uncomfortable, whereas laughter is considered an acceptable outlet.

Laughter yoga is not yoga in the traditional sense (thank fuck because I can barely touch my shins let alone my toes). The 'yoga' label comes from the breathing exercises. It's important to remember that laughter yoga focuses on laughter, not humour. So, there are no jokes in the Zoom, just a series of exercises that involved laughing out loud in a rhythm. Fake, loud laughter. Does it feel weird? YES. I feel like a right dick for the first few minutes. It's a vulnerable experience, that would make even the most confident person feel awkward. But after a while, this fades away (and not just because I turned my camera off). I feel giddy and strange. Then the laughter stops being fake and is suddenly real. My body is racked with animated giggles, and my stomach muscles contract from the effort. *What on earth is happening? What am I laughing at?* It's very pleasant, just as laughter always is. So I decide to go with it.

Later, I talk to Louise Gates, a pioneer in the field of yoga and mental health. She is in the process of completing the first PhD assessing the impact of laughter yoga on mental health.

We talk about why it specifically helps for anxiety and panic attacks. 'Think of it like a cardio exercise,' she tells me. 'A good laughing session will help to burn off any excess cortisol and adrenaline. It also regulates your breathing, which is always an issue with panic attacks.' I think of myself hyperventilating, desperately trying to swallow more air, which only seems to worsen the attack. Whereas laughter keeps breathing consistent but steady, thereby ensuring that equal parts of both oxygen and carbon dioxide remain in the bloodstream.

Another random fact about me. I. Fucking. HATE. Mindfulness. The same applies for meditation, transcendental meditation and some aspects of hypnotherapy. Basically, all of the holistic therapies that are supposed to improve anxiety and panic. Why? Two reasons really, I can't do them, and I can't be arsed doing them. They don't work for me, no matter how hard I try. Ask me to 'focus on my breathing', and I WILL hyperventilate. Guaranteed. There's too much pressure to be calm and 'empty your mind of all thoughts'. Unfortunately, I'm not wired that way and practising them makes me feel like a failure. They're even harder to deploy during a panic attack. As Louise comments, 'Lots of the traditional breathing exercises demand that the person be still, when during a panic attack that's the last thing you want to do.'

Laughter yoga is, in many ways, the lazy person's mindfulness. Zero focus or effort needed, just laugh. I was delighted to find something that worked for me, rather than something that sometimes worked, if I could get in the zone. 'Fake laughter is proven to become real laughter within thirty seconds,' Louise tells me. The body can't differentiate between genuine laughter and just making the sounds. So a person will experience the benefits either way.

Humour as a tool

Where laughter yoga helps to ease the physical symptoms of an attack, I find humour helps with the mental/emotional symptoms.

Comedy is a short-term way to lose contact with reality as it provides a distance from pain and danger. Or as author Jon P. Hatcher states: 'it provides a unique and unrivalled perspective that shifts our thinking away from despair and toward the awareness that a radically different outcome is possible. Humour is the most accessible form of relief.'[6] A panic attack is a miscalculation of danger, one that takes the mind out of reality and traps it in a prison filled with spikes. Humour is similar in terms of taking us out of reality, but the prison it dumps us in is more of a soft bouncy castle, one that triggers a sense of joy rather than terror.

'When used appropriately, humour can have a place in therapy for generalised anxiety disorder, panic, depression, and social anxiety. It can be a part of interpersonal therapy and CBT.'[7]

When I talk once again to panic master David Carbonell about this, he agrees and furthermore highlights that humour is a powerful way to deal with the trash talk (see page 79) that can accompany a panic attack. 'It's a great way to steer clear of becoming embroiled with these thoughts. Simply take the thought, agree with it and then add some exaggerated details of your own.' Wendy had unknowingly helped me to do this when she joked that I should jump on the table if I was going to take my top off. This was proof that humour could be deployed as a coping technique. I started to think of it as a 'reverse panic trick', a way to blindside the amygdala and release the tension. Further to easing distress and as a therapeutic tool, jokes have a way of making shitty topics more accessible.

During most conversations with people who haven't themselves experienced anxiety or panic, there's usually an element of discomfort. I can sense it, see it in their eyes and read it in their body language. They can't relate and are afraid to cause offence, but also desperate to change the subject. More often it tends to be previous generations who think that one should, 'keep that sort of thing to yourself'.

If this occurs and I sense discomfort, then I will try to make the person laugh. Not to make light of the condition, but rather to communicate that everything is OK. It's an approach that I've been criticised for in the past, but I stand by it. I'd argue that we can't expect everyone to be wholly comfortable with something they've never experienced. Or as my mate Aaron said to me: 'Obviously, some subjects aren't there to be made fun of, but if we can underpin an extremely serious subject with a hint of levity it makes it more accessible.' Taking the piss or making a joke is a way to make the other person feel more comfortable. It's a safe space from which we can build. If they're relaxed, then they're more likely to take in what you say or even learn something.

Gabriel Nathan, editor-in-chief of *OC87 Recovery Diaries*, uses humour in his documentary *A Man, A Bug, and A Mission*, in which he and his 1963 Volkswagen Beetle Herbie the Love Bug replica depart on a 1,100-mile road trip up and down the east coast of America, encouraging others to share their stories about suicide and spreading awareness of the National Suicide Prevention Lifeline (1–800–273-TALK). Gabe is a quirky guy, with a razor-sharp wit. We bond at the OC87 writer's retreat over our shared experiences and love of the cult TV show *Father Ted*. Of all the difficult mental health topics, suicide trumps the lot, making it difficult to start conversations. 'I believe what makes people uncomfortable when talking about suicide is fear,' he tells me and I'd have to agree. From my experience with panic, I know that fear is an emotion that doesn't sit well with us. We don't like to talk about the things we're afraid of, things that could take our loved ones from us. Gabe also used to work at a psychiatric hospital and mentioned that the staff liked to joke all the time. 'There is a reason that dark humour is so delicious, why it feels so good to laugh at something naughty or subversive, because we're not supposed to, so the joke feels doubly good, because it is an act of rebellion.' An act of rebellion that allows us to shine a light on horrific topics and discuss them openly.

Laughter is a huge part of my life, both from a therapeutic perspective and general wellbeing. It's a lifeline that I deploy tactically when I'm caught in the raging seas of a panic attack.

At a recent conference, I knew that panic was going to make an appearance as soon as I got out of my car. I was tired and had started my period that morning. I was due to give a talk in front of a sports hall full of people; not just any sort of people – educators. For some reason, teachers really intimidate me. I think it's the whole 'position of authority from my past' thing – I turn back into a twelve-year-old who might at any moment piss herself on stage. Sarah, the liaison, meets me at reception and we sneak into the back of the hall. Another person is finishing their presentation. I estimate an audience of around 200 people. *SHIT.* I let the situation get the better of me and decide that my entire working future now depends on this one talk. *How will you escape if you freak out?* panic whispers. *This room is huge! It'll take five minutes to leg it back to the door!* I feel the familiar warm current flowing through my veins and my limbs felt numb. I take a few belly breaths and try to stabilise. I can't handle this. Why did I think I could? I don't care about returning the money, I just want to leave before something awful happens.

In a moment of clarity, I turn to Sarah, who up until this point I've never met in my life, and explain what was happening. 'I'm having a panic attack. It's all OK, but could you possibly tell me a joke, or something funny?' I expect her to look shocked, or frown. After all, how unprofessional must I appear? She surprises me: 'This morning I walked all the way from the bus stop to school with my skirt tucked in my knickers. It's a fifteen-minute walk, so you think that at some point I would've noticed the cold air on my bum cheeks! I only realised when a cabbie pulled over and shouted: "Nice bloomers, love!" I'm wearing very large knickers today.' I feel the corners of my mouth twitch and we both start giggling. A perfect anecdote to fear. The panic retreats, like a shadow creeping back into the dark.

CHAPTER 6

Social Events, Panic and the Rule of Opposites

'When you experience a panic attack, try and be consciously aware of your gut reaction ... and then do the complete opposite.'

– Dr David Carbonell

It's a Thursday night and I'm standing outside a house that isn't my own. It's freezing and the ground beneath my feet sparkles with frost. I tread lightly out of instinct. As an adult, falling takes a lot longer to recover from, both physically and psychologically. Last year for instance, I slipped getting out of my parents' shower and dragged the curtain down with me. (Shockingly it did not hold my weight.) I fell in a seated position and landed on the nearby toilet, the shower curtain draped over me like a tent. I was lucky to get away with nothing more than a sore arse and a mild case of shower trauma. It took me weeks to get over it, and I was extra careful in any bathroom environment, whereas twenty years ago I'd have forgotten about the whole experience within half an hour.

I keep my footing light, mindful of the black ice hidden on the pavement. A fall here would be painful. I shudder, my ears are stinging, and I cover them instinctively to ease the pain. One drink after work turned into several, as it usually did. Time flies when I'm knocking back cheap red wine and talking shit with my friend Kate. After missing the last tube, it made sense to crash at her place, though I'm regretting it now and as she fumbles in her bag, I feel irritated. *She'd better be looking for her keys and not a cigarette.* I've seen this woman beg, actually beg, a Sainsbury's security guard to let her in five minutes before closing time. She reasoned that smoking is a 'legal addiction' and was he so heartless as to deny her the tobacco that would get her through the night? He was, yes. Although he did offer her one out of his own pack.

'Christ, will you hurry up, I'm dying!' I hiss.

She raises her middle finger but doesn't look up. 'About normal for you then.'

The cold air bites my skin. 'Remind me again why I keep you in my life?'

'Because there are few people in this world who will listen patiently while you bang on about Greek mythology, or pasty barms, or the importance of retinol in skincare, or whatever random shit pops into your head! And besides all that, we're both crazy!'

It's true: among other things, we'd spent a large part of the evening talking about her OCD and my anxiety.

Six months before this night, Kate got it in her head that because she'd smoked a cigarette while walking past a petrol station, it had obviously blown up, therefore making her responsible for the deaths of everyone on site. She reasoned that she hadn't heard the explosion because she had her headphones on. This incident is how we became friends. Not because she blew me up at a petrol station, but because I noticed she was ringing an unknown person several times one morning and asking random questions such as: 'Do you sell milk?' or 'Is there a Costa Coffee machine?' (We worked on the Strand, making the availability of milk or coffee a non-issue.) It turns out she was ringing the petrol station to 'make sure they weren't dead' or that she 'couldn't hear police sirens in the background'.

The door finally opens, and we crash into the hallway together. My breath comes out like steam, swirling in front of my face. 'Fuck, I think it's actually colder in here than outside!' Instinctively, I wrap my arms across my body and squeeze tight, holding my muscles tense.

'That makes it worse you know,' she says, stabbing in the alarm code.

'What?'

She points at my chest. 'Holding your muscles stiff like that. It reduces the blood flow and takes longer to warm up.'

'Is that true?' I ask, surprised.

She doesn't answer and moves quickly into the kitchen with her phone. I suspect she's on the Pizza Hut app, the thing we both said we wouldn't do two hours ago, but it's a dead cert now.

Dumping my bag on the floor I stumble after her. 'So why is that my natural response then, if it's wrong?'

She shrugs. 'The brain doesn't always get it right. Think about alcohol, or junk food.'

'Or smoking like a chimney?' I interrupt.

I receive the finger once again. 'Stuffed crust yeah?'

I don't answer; she knows better than to ask stupid questions.

I lay awake in bed that night, thinking about what she'd said and regretting consuming that final slice of pizza. If my instincts about keeping myself warm were wrong, then could that be the case for panic also? After all, nothing my brain ever screamed at me during an attack seemed to be useful.

During this period, I'd been having difficulties in social situations. Dinners, parties, work events – it didn't matter, the routine was always the same. I'd arrive sweating buckets and within minutes I'd be hiding in the toilets or on my way back to the nearest tube station. Randomly, the use of my name seemed to be triggering the attacks. If a person said my name directly – for example, 'CLAIRE, how is work going?' or 'You're vegetarian right, CLAIRE?' – my brain, already on edge, would suddenly backfire and I'd be hurled into a state of panic. *Say something, you dick! Say anything.* In response, I'd abruptly excuse myself (in my trademark Jane Austen voice obviously) and leave.

It was humiliating and, where possible, I'd avoid going out altogether. I couldn't explain what was happening and I felt so let down by my instincts. I was desperate to be normal and actually enjoy a social interaction.

Up until this point, I'd been confident that my brain was the ultimate authority on what I needed; it didn't make poor judgement calls. But now I began to wonder. I'd already established that the amygdala couldn't always distinguish a genuinely dangerous situation from a non-threatening one. I knew the trash talk that popped into my head during an attack wasn't an indicator of my immediate death, that in reality it was a just another symptom of panic. Therefore, I wondered, was my body being tricked into behaving in ways that were counterproductive?

As I mentioned, if I had a panic attack at a party, for example, my brain would instruct me to 'run away!' or 'hide!' If I followed the instructions the attack would ease initially, but rather than being relieved, I'd feel embarrassed and ashamed. I didn't feel safe, as the voice of panic had promised, instead I felt like a failure who'd been conned, and this simply made things worse. Reacting the way that I had confirmed to my amygdala that it was right to trigger a panic attack, because I was indeed in a dangerous situation. In fact, the next time that I found myself in a similar environment, another, usually more intense attack would be triggered. *We already established that this place is a threat. Why have you come back, you lunatic!*

'Always trust your instincts, they are messages from your soul.' I read this on a poster once, when I was waiting to go on stage at an educational conference. I thought: *I fucking hope not because my instincts are telling me to jump through the stained-glass window on my left.* In my opinion, a lot of inspirational quotes are missing a set of terms and conditions. For example, when you spy a glossy advert for a product in a magazine and they've squeezed around 200 words into the T&Cs at the bottom in really tiny font? For example: Unless you look like the woman in this photo then the product won't work, and even if it does, you can never hope to have skin like hers. So, the terms and conditions for the above quote might be something like: Unless your instincts are similar to Claire Eastham's. In which case, you might want to drop by the doctor's surgery … and grab a hot chocolate on your way home to soften the blow. Only make sure the hot chocolate is from Upper Crust rather than Starbucks because the Starbucks one is shit and will put you in a mood for hours. Seriously, you'll be livid.

Was this just me with dodgy instincts? I asked my followers on Twitter whether panic attacks made them behave in ways that were counterproductive and received the following responses:

As soon as I feel it, I freeze and don't move a muscle. I know from experience that gentle movement helps to ease the attack, but I can't bring myself to do it. My brain screams at me to remain rigid. So, I hold myself tense, and remain trapped inside my own personal hell!

– Ayesha, Birmingham

I avoid situations that have triggered panic attacks in the past. Believe me I've tried to go back and face my demons, but the sensations are so overwhelming that I can't bring myself to do it. I have an urge to flee and save myself, even from a friend's birthday dinner at Pizza Express! Last I checked that place wasn't dangerous, but my brain believes otherwise.

– Brian, Cheshire

I have to run. I can't put it more straightforwardly than that. If a panic attack strikes, then I will leave any situation no matter how awkward. I can't NOT obey my brain.

– Kirsty, London

It seems as though there are a few of us out there acting batshit crazy because it feels natural to us.

Biologist Dr David Bainbridge states that our reactions to fear are not only primitive, but a result of cognitive development. Humans made it to the top of the food chain because of how quickly our brains identify and react to danger, our three key reactions to threats being fight, flight or freeze.

This means that during a panic attack, my urge to run away from social situations was quite literally textbook. The brain behaves exactly as it should, as it's programmed to do when danger is identified, just as a healthy, functioning bladder alerts us when we need urinate, to avoid pissing one's pants. It's remarkable when you think about it, the body just does its job without any input from us, why shouldn't we be impressed by that? Sadly, rather than being stunned by the sophistication of our fight-or-flight response we feel embarrassed and frustrated because it's been triggered in error, at Grandma's sixtieth birthday party for example. This was very difficult for me to accept for many reasons.

For one thing I'm a spontaneous person, some might even say reckless. I've been known to jump into fountains (Trafalgar Square fountains at midnight, to be precise, and no, it wasn't worth it). I've gone to random parties at 11 p.m. and spent £180 on a theatre ticket, because I wanted to see Kit Harington in the flesh; the idea was that even though I was engaged at the time, if Kit noticed me on stage and thought, 'Wow, she's fit, we should probably cop off after the show,' that was allowed, because it was a once-in-a-lifetime opportunity. Dan has a similar arrangement with Emma Stone. We're both yet to succeed.

My instincts for what I want tend to be strong, as is knowing immediately what I like and what I don't like. I chose my wedding dress in under sixty seconds. I knew it was the one when I saw it (Mum made me try on three other dresses first, as in fairness she'd travelled all the way from Bolton). We made an offer on our house from the car as we drove away from the first viewing. I knew that I wanted to write from the age of eight and I always knew that I'd have a canine by my side as soon as I could afford to keep her. (Seriously, I put together a PowerPoint presentation to convince both my husband and our landlord. That's not being organised, it's obsessive determination. I *would* have a dog.) It's a quality that my husband admires, 'You know what you want and don't mess about. I love that your instincts are so strong.'

So, imagine my horror at discovering that my internal compass is completely fucked when it comes to panic and danger.

When people say 'when you know, you just know', they're usually referring to finding a soulmate. For me, on the other hand, it's a reaction to a potentially threatening environment: 'When I know that I have to run, trust me *I know*.' Panic takes over and it's normally in a situation that would be deemed inappropriate. As Dr Soph highlights: 'The systems of fight or flight have escalated so strongly that you have this moment where you're totally overwhelmed. A peak in anxiety symptoms where everything feels lost.' Lost and overwhelmed are the *exact* emotions that I feel while in the grips of a panic attack. It's as though I'm being pulled in a hundred different directions, unsure of the right path or how to respond appropriately.

An example of this would be at the hairdresser, an environment that I can deal with now but used to dread. The bright lights, the noise, the pressure to be entertaining and interesting for the person cutting my hair (who I'm sure has no expectations). I don't like strangers touching me at the best of times, so the intimacy that comes with letting someone run their fingers through your hair made me cringe. The whole experience made me feel vulnerable. On one occasion, when trimming my fringe, the hairdresser rested the blade of the scissors against my face, the tops of my eyelids to be precise, as she slowly inched across. Even now, I can feel the cool of the metal. She could blind me if she chose to. I was at her mercy. I held my breath as I always did, feeling that somehow this was safer, and remained frozen to the spot. *If I just keep still and don't breathe, then everything will be fine.* The muscles in my upper body ached in protest and my heart was pounding. The hairdresser chatted away to her friend as she worked, cutting and then stopping to emphasise a point in her conversation. *If you move, you'll die.* I needed to move, I needed to breathe, why couldn't she just finish! The next time she turned her head, I lost it. Jumped up and screamed: 'PLEASE! Will you get that blade away from my fucking face!'

Silence fell over the salon, and the hairdresser gazed at me in horror. My heart was pounding and my whole body trembled with exertion. Why had I reacted so aggressively? The 'normal' response would've been to calmly explain that having my fringe cut made me nervous and could she cut it as fast as possible? Yet, my brain had chosen to 'freeze' and then when that wasn't successful, to 'fight'.

Fortunately, Charlie could see past my outburst and responded with kindness. 'Are you all right, babe?' she asked, and after apologising profusely I blurted out that I had anxiety and having my hair cut stresses me out. I was fighting to hold back tears of humiliation. 'You should've said something, ya daft sod! I hate to think of you being so uncomfortable.' One of her assistants got me a cup of tea and we finished the haircut. She's still my hairdresser as it turns out and also a good mate. When trimming my fringe these days she always 'checks in' to make sure I'm breathing!

Now what? Safety behaviours

All right, so I'd recognised that a panic attack was a trick. A catastrophic misinterpretation of what's happening in the body. This was comforting to an extent, knowing that, despite what panic said, I wasn't about to die or go nuts.

Yet, that knowledge didn't help me to act correctly or, even better, stop the attacks from happening. Just knowing about 'the panic trick' wasn't enough any more. I didn't want to simply 'get through' a panic attack, now I was determined to cut their duration in half or find ways to make myself feel more comfortable while they passed.

My pilgrimage into the world of opposites begins when I meet Professor John Powell. I interviewed him for the charity MQ, as part of their award-winning podcast series: *Open Mind*. MQ is a revolutionary charity that funds research into mental illness. As an ambassador, I'm fortunate to have access to many of their ongoing research projects.

Btw, can I please take a moment to say that I think scientists and researchers are genuine superheroes. When I was first diagnosed with my condition, I was told – in so many words – that there was very little that could be done to help me. Even now, almost a decade later, very little has changed with regard to treatment. That's fucked up. Ten years without progression. In fact, during my last appointment the doctor sighed and said, 'You know more about this than we do now. There's nothing else I can prescribe you or suggest.' I appreciated his candour, but it didn't soften the blow. I'd just come out of hospital at the time.

When I was first diagnosed, the lack of treatment was a harsh reality to accept. I was scared and felt abandoned by the national institution I trusted to take care of me. The one that I proudly paid my taxes to support.

One of the first things I learn from MQ is this: 'For every person diagnosed with mental illness in the UK, £8 is spent on research. To put this into context, for cancer it's £138.' This was a sobering fact to hear. Like cancer, mental illness steals lives. In fact, according to the Mental Health Foundation: 'Suicide is the biggest killer of men under the age of forty-five.'

Discovering MQ was a real galvanising moment. The majority of mental health charities focus on spreading awareness, whereas MQ were actively seeking cures. Which after being told for so long that there is no cure for mental illness was incredible. There were people out there actively seeking new treatments and dedicating their lives to understanding more about the brain. MQ seek to save and change lives through science.

Through the charity, I have been introduced to many researchers, one of who is Jon.

During our interview, he talks to me about panic attack 'safety behaviours' and aptly points out a few of mine. I presumed that 'safety behaviour' fell into the category of 'avoidance' whereby a person deliberately avoids a situation through fear of having a panic attack. However, I learn through Jon that they can be more subtle and therefore go undetected. Until this point, for example, I hadn't realised that I hold my body rigid when I'm nervous, sucking in my stomach muscles and clenching my fists. 'You're bracing your body for battle!' Jon smiles. I suppose I was, but it's something that I've always done, I didn't even think about it. I hold my body stiff to 'remain in control' and feel safe.

He explains that safety behaviours are essentially habits that we develop in response to panic and anxiety. 'During a panic attack you may have randomly behaved in a certain way and you didn't die, therefore the brain associates that behaviour with "saving you".' This would explain why some people who experience panic attacks need to have gum with them at all time, or a bottle of water. However, my 'safety behaviours' were counterproductive. Holding my body stiff prevented the blood from flowing to my muscles and oxygen from entering my lungs, which triggered hyperventilation. Nadiya Hussain had a similar tactic. She told me that during *Bake Off* she would snap an elastic band against her wrist whenever she felt panic rising. This gives a whole new meaning to the phrase 'snap out of it'! For the record, no, it didn't help, and she was left with very raw skin.

I also know a guy who clenches his bum cheeks during public-speaking events, because he's adamant that this staves off an attack. 'I do it and it works,' he quips. 'I know it's ridiculous, but I'm afraid to stop.' Buns of steel indeed.

More extreme examples of safety behaviours would include excessive use of alcohol or drugs (illegal or prescription), for example, drinking a bottle of wine when the first sniff of panic arrives. Humans have a terrible track record of self-medicating to avoid all levels of discomfort. Although, is it really that surprising, considering the lack of suitable treatments?

When I research safety behaviours in more detail, I realise that one of mine developed at the young age of twelve. I was regularly told off for daydreaming in maths class. Teachers presumed it was because I found the subject boring, when actually it was because I didn't understand and panicked. All of my friends seemed to be following the lesson, so if I didn't, then I was obviously an idiot. The idea of being outed an idiot sent me into a state of panic. So, I'd drift in and out of various fantasy worlds. 'Daydreaming is a way of staying "inside your head" and not really being involved in what is going on around you. Although you might feel less anxious, if you stop daydreaming and start engaging, the anxiety will return.' Yep, this about sums it up. Thank you, Arlin Cuncic, author of *The Anxiety Workbook*. For all these years, I thought it was procrastination and I'm sure in some circumstances, it is. Daydreaming in particular crops up when I'm stressed about an important writing deadline. For instance, fantasising about how I'd look with a shaved head is preferable to dealing with the worry that my work is shit and I'm going to lose everything (which, in turn, triggers a panic attack).

If these behaviours become ingrained, then how do we change them? I talk to clinical psychologist Dr Andrea Reinecke about this and the controversial treatment that she deploys (again funded by MQ). I knew that both Andrea and her treatment were right up my street when I hear that she locks patients in a cupboard. YES! Anything eccentric and I'm all over it. We talk on the phone and I quiz her about her various panic research projects.

'Experimental research has confirmed that during the presentation of threatening images, anxious participants are more likely to use dysfunctional regulation strategies such as suppression or cognitive avoidance. In contrast, they are less likely to use adaptive, successful techniques such as positive reappraisal. In further support of the idea of anxiety disorders being associated with an increase rather than a decrease in neural responses associated with affect regulation, CBT has been shown to lead to a decrease in responsivity in prefrontal brain areas usually implicated in cognitive control.'

Basically, Andrea summarises that if participants have even the smallest opportunity to distance themselves from fear or discomfort, then they will. Distraction is a common strategy, e.g. checking their phone. This slows down progress, as the amygdala may be placated initially, but the issue with panic remains. She argues that the only way to achieve long-lasting change is to force participants to experience the symptoms of panic.

In her experiment, Andrea locks patients in a cupboard because she believes that this is the most direct way to communicate with the amygdala. She sends me two of her published papers to read: 'The 2015 paper shows that patients with panic disorder have a much more sensitive amygdala than healthy volunteers (they respond to the same negative images with much more activation in this area, which is responsible for threat detection and processing). The 2018 paper shows that this amygdala oversensitivity in these patients can be resolved within four sessions of exposure-based CBT.' The study is still ongoing, but it would appear that the cupboard has great power! 'There are no distractions in the cupboard, no opportunity for the patient to avoid the attack. It gives them a chance to accept the attack and learn how to manage it without the use of safety behaviours.'

To put this into context, I conducted my own exposure therapy and it took nine months to notice real results. A few sessions with Andrea may have changed my life, or at least made me feel less alone. My so-called 'safety behaviours' had prevented me from discovering that although horrendous, I could survive a panic attack.

Taking action

If my brain could not be trusted during a panic attack, then the option going forward must be to oppose it. A mutiny of sorts. Simple enough in theory, but a bitch in practice. When it believes we're in danger, the amygdala will not go quietly into the night. Like a dictator holding on to his last grips of power.

From experience, I knew that my instincts would be the following:

- Sucking my stomach in and holding my entire body tense
- Holding my breath
- Trying to distract myself with my phone
- Leaving the situation, whether by hiding in the toilets, or exiting the venue completely

As Andrea informs me, 'Knowing how you'll behave is a positive. There will be no surprises.' I reasoned that having advance knowledge of my behaviour would help me to do the complete opposite during an attack and that although my instincts felt accurate, I needed to flip them.

I put this into practice one week later at a dinner with family and friends. I told Dan my plan in advance, to ensure that I had backup, and I also prepared some breathing techniques.

I dreaded the evening all day, hoping that despite previous social occasions, panic wouldn't make an appearance, even though I knew that this would be counterproductive. As the waiter arrived to take our drinks order, I felt the first wave hit. *This is a terrible idea. Why did you think you could do it?* my brain screamed. *You should leave now, nobody will judge you, they all know that you struggle in social situations. We can try again another time. It's too soon.* I had the overwhelming urge to cry and I was desperate to flee. I couldn't do this.

I'd written down something that David Carbonell told me and stuck it in my blazer pocket, hoping it would help: 'choose long-term freedom over short-term discomfort'. Taking a few belly breaths, I used these words as an anchor. I was uncomfortable, *not* in danger. By this point the physical symptoms were raging: pounding heart, sweating, dizziness. I turned to Dan and said, 'I feel like I'm going to shit myself or start screaming!'

He squeezed my hand. 'Sounds about right! But you know what this is. You know that it's a trick and although you feel bad now, it will eventually ease if you stay put.'

He was right. This was natural, everything that was happening was a result of panic and nothing more. I started my breathing techniques and told myself, *All right, if you still feel this bad in sixty seconds then you can leave. But if you feel even 1 per cent better then you have to stay another sixty seconds.* By three minutes, the attack started to dissipate. It had worked. I was euphoric to the extent of being manic, 'I didn't go mad and I didn't shit myself!' I announced to Dan. He clinked my glass in response. 'Happy days!' Once again, I'd taken back some power from panic.

CHAPTER 7

Who's Flying this Plane? Airports and Travel

The first time that Grandma Eastham went abroad on holiday (rather than somewhere in the UK) was a disaster. It was the early nineties, and she and Grandad booked a week in Spain. Up until that year, Grandma had travelled exclusively by coach, or whatever old banger my grandad had managed to acquire on the cheap. A favourite family story being when such an old banger caught fire on the way back from their holiday in Weymouth and Grandad had to put it out with a two-litre bottle of lemonade, as Grandma sat on the side of the motorway, eating custard creams and shouting abuse at him.

The night before they flew, she didn't sleep at all, sitting instead on the front steps of the house, rocking back and forth and chain-smoking cigarettes. 'I'm going to die tomorrow,' she thought, 'I'm actually going to die.' God knows how they got her to the airport and through check-in. Still, when finally persuaded to board the plane, she was outraged when Grandad fastened his own seatbelt before hers, in her mind definitive proof that after forty years of marriage, he didn't care about her. She refused to speak to him for three days, which I suspect the man was secretly pleased about!

Things went from bad to batshit very quickly. After take-off she began shouting at fellow passengers who got out of their seats to use the toilet. 'Sit down!' she yelled, fearing they'd rock the plane and make it fall out of the sky. She refused to eat, drink, or do a cross-word, and instead just sat hyperventilating and gripping her seat. I like to think that Grandad tried to comfort her at some point, but then knowing my grandma, she'd have probably torn a strip off him for even breathing.

Eventually, a thoughtful air steward brought one of the pilots over to try and calm her nerves.

The conversation went something like this:

Air steward: Mrs Eastham, everything is fine. I've brought Mr Shaw to talk to you.
Grandma: Why is that helpful? Who is he?
Mr Shaw: I'm the pilot, madam.
Grandma: Oh my god, if you're the pilot, who's flying the sodding plane?!!

The similarities between my grandma and me are uncanny. We both react to fear with angry outbursts and spontaneous action. I can't say I blame her for acting the way that she did, because flying is scary! How can anybody be cool with the fact that they're sitting in a tin cylinder 30,000 feet in the air?

I've lost count of the times that I've sobbed uncontrollably on planes (before sertraline), hiding behind my sunglasses.

The worst experience had to be our honeymoon. After the com-mercial flight landed, we flew to the tiny Maldives island via seaplane. Dan kept this vital piece of information from me until everything was booked, which was definitely for the best. In case you're wondering, a seaplane is exactly what it sounds like. A cabin (if you can even call it that), barely big enough for six people, takes off on the water and lands on the water.

As Dan sat enjoying the posh, exclusive longue, I watched the tiny plane being fuelled, and fretted. 'You must be so excited!' gushed a flight attendant. I faked a smile and then went back to my fretting. What is it about extreme activities that prompt others to congratulate you? 'You're jumping off a cliff? That's amazing, you must be buzzing!' 'Wow, you're flying in a tin bath over the Indian Ocean, without a seatbelt? That's awesome!'

When the time came to board, Dan had to semi-wrestle me down the jetty, and if I'm being totally honest, my biggest motivation for climbing on board was money. (As in we'd spent a HUGE amount of money on this holiday, so I was bloody well going to experience it, even at the risk of death.) Money has always been a shameless motivator for me. I know this isn't something you're supposed to admit, particularly as an author. It's expected that we're motivated by the love of the art, but seriously, fuck that, I want to be able to afford things.

For instance, money is the only reason I did a trapeze jump for *Top Santé* magazine in 2014 (I was working on a freelance piece investigating 'unusual' exercise activities). I don't have a fear of heights per se, but neither am I fond of jumping from them, as everyone in the vicinity discovered. *You're going to be the person who dies in some kind of freak accident.* It wasn't my proudest moment, telling the guy in charge of trapeze safety that if he let me fall before I was ready, I'd 'climb back up these fucking ladders and *twat* you. Nobody else, mate, just YOU!' Still, they were paying me £500 to write about it and that money would allow me to get my dog, so, of course I bloody jumped, death or not. He was very sweet about the whole thing afterwards. 'Fear affects people in different ways.' He smiled, accepting my mortified apologies.

The seaplane was another level of fear entirely. For starters it's not as though I could threaten to twat the pilots if they dared to crash.

Words could never really express the level of noise in that tin cabin. Think the T-Rex from *Jurassic Park* crossed with a pneumatic drill. I still shudder thinking about it.

The pre-flight conversation went like this:

Me: Oh my god, the pilot doesn't even have shoes on.
Dan: Yeah that's good, babe. He can probably feel the pedals better without shoes.
Me: Oh, fuck off!

One of the pilots was also checking his Nokia 3310 phone, and for some reason this disturbed me more than his lack of footwear. How could he fly a sophisticated piece of technology when he still used a 3310?!

Just when I thought the noise couldn't get any louder, the plane began to move and nothing else could be heard. It was all-consuming and assaulted my ears. Hands down, I've never been that frightened in my entire life. For once, the panic was justified and rather than paying attention to my pounding heart, I focused on the possibility of my impending doom.

As we left the water I started screaming at the top of my lungs: *'Oh my god! Oh my fucking god, we're going to die, we're all going to die. Arrrggghhhhh!'*

Dan didn't hear a word of this. Nobody did. My screams were drowned out by the roar of the engine.

When we landed, I staggered off the plane and into the arms of the woman holding a welcome garland. Then asked to be taken to our hut, because I was sure I would throw up. Then I had two shots of tequila, as Dan tucked into a Wispa Gold, delighted that chocolate was included in the free mini bar.

Flying is so difficult for people who live with panic or anxiety because it's an experience that cannot be controlled. All passengers put their lives in the hands of the pilot, crew and, to a certain extent, fate. Zero control is a panic attack nightmare. As I mentioned, I don't even trust my hairdresser with my fringe, so why would I be fine trusting my life to a complete stranger, who I can't see?

In general, flying is one of the most common fears; aviophobia affects millions of people with degrees of severity. According to recent statistics, 'between 33 and 40 per cent of all people experience some form of anxiety when it comes to flying'.[1]

In the summer months, most blog requests I receive ask for me to cover 'flying anxiety' or 'how to stay calm on an aeroplane'.

This makes sense. It's not what would be considered an irrational phobia, such as pogonophobia (a fear of beards), or alektorophobia (a fear of chickens). Both of which are unlikely to kill a person in the UK. Whereas, on a plane you're technically in a high-risk situation that could harm you.

Aeroplanes and airports are well-known stressors, even for those who don't experience panic attacks. From the queuing and bright lights, to the noise and inevitable fumbling with passports, every aspect is an attack on the senses. Tensions and emotions run high for every person.

Psychologist Philip Karahassan writes about the physiological and emotional effects of the whole flying experience. 'Firstly, you have had to get up, usually early, and then make sure you have everything ready to go. Then you have the long journey to the airport and then check-in which can be a long wait.'[2] Plus, if you're anything like my husband then you probably haven't had more than two hours sleep anyway. The night before a holiday he gets paranoid about sleeping through not one, but all three of the alarms we've set.

'I hate airports. From the moment I arrive I feel like I've done something wrong, as though I'm going to be told off by a member of staff or asked to leave. I feel angry that I've paid so much money to be herded around like cattle. This is not something that I would accept in any other situation. The whole thing is stressful and not an ideal start for a holiday.'
  – Helen

The security checks are especially frantic. I've never smuggled an illegal item in my entire life. Yet, inevitably, while waiting for my turn to go through the body scanner, I convince myself that I've somehow packed a gun or I'm carrying a sack of cocaine. *Should I smile, or should I look serious? How's my posture? How would a guilty person look? I'm definitely going to get arrested.* By this point the guard is waving me through and I try my best not to look overtly relieved. Then, there's the mad scramble at the end, trying to get all your shit back in your bag at great speed as the trays come flying past.

A panic attack on a flight is inevitable for me and usually occurs around thirty minutes after take-off. That's when the knowledge than I'm stuck here for the duration kicks in and nothing can be done, making me feel trapped. I know how to handle it now, but it can still be an uncomfortable experience if I don't prepare.

The big trip

When I was asked by online publication *OC87 Recovery Diaries* to be a guest at their writing retreat in New Jersey USA, I was chuffed to bits. I'd written an article for them the year before and had maintained a good relationship with the editor-in-chief Gabriel Nathan (see page 101). He was putting together a retreat for women, an opportunity for attendees to talk about their mental health and express it via writing. There would be workshops, talks, stress-free networking, not to mention the beautiful beach which was a two-minute walk from the hotel. I like to think that Gabe asked me to attend because I'm an inspirational woman and not just because of the aforementioned shared love of *Father Ted*. He also wanted me to take part in the documentary being filmed over the course of the weekend. For a whole five minutes I was thrilled. With the exception of Disney World, I'd never been to the US. This was an incredible opportunity! I could spend time around people who discussed their mental health openly and maybe make some new friends (not to mention the pancakes I'd get to eat).

After accepting the invitation, the reality of what I'd agreed to do set in very quickly. *That's a nine-hour flight.* I hadn't done anything like that in years and never alone. Was it feasible, could I really do it? Nine hours there and nine hours back?

Flying is a known trigger of panic attacks, even for those who have never previously experienced one. My own brother, who is more chilled than an ice-cube tray, had one on a flight back from Spain. 'I think I had one of those things you get, sis,' he told me. 'I was too hot, and I couldn't sit still. This woman next to me was banging on about something and I just lost it. I had to get out.' (It probably didn't help that he was travelling back from a stag do and extremely hungover.) After rising from his seat, he rushed to the toilet, stripped off all his clothes and drenched himself in cold water. 'I stayed locked in there until my heart stopped pounding. Something was wrong, but I didn't know what. Even when I sat back down, I was counting the minutes until the plane landed.'

This isn't the first tale I've heard about people experiencing their first attack in the sky. The environment on board is unfamiliar and breaks with the comfortable routine that an individual is used to. The brain is naturally on high alert.

I made a snap decision about New Jersey in the end. I hadn't let panic control my life so far and I wasn't planning to do so now. (This is a romantic way of saying, 'I had a glass of wine and thought, fuck it!') This was a once-in-a-lifetime opportunity and, if nothing else, it was a chance to experience panic attacks in the air and learn how to cope with them. My instincts were telling me not to go, so based on the rule of opposites I was absolutely going.

Six months later and I find myself on the plane, furiously searching for space in the overhead compartment for my bag. This is arguably the most stressful part of any flight and a task that I normally leave to Dan. I open the compartment above my head to find it completely full with suitcases. Great. I immediately HATE everyone on board.

Air steward: There's no more room, madam. Give your bag to me and we'll try and store it someplace else.
Me: Oh no, it's fine, I'll just shove it under my seat. (Grips bag like a small child.)

Air steward: I'm afraid you can't do that, madam.

Me: Right. The thing is, unless you want to see a grown woman freaking out in a hysterical manner, then you'll allow me to keep my bag.

People are staring and I can feel my skin starting to heat with embarrassment. *You seem crazy. I knew this would happen. You're either going to lose custody of your bag for nine hours or get kicked off the plane. They'll think you're drunk and send the police on board to drag you off.* Fortunately, after a few moments of excruciating silence, a kind man in a seat across the aisle offers to move his bag down a bit and places mine in the locker. LEGEND. Small gestures make a huge difference. Like, for example, when someone lets you go in front of them at the supermarket tills, or you get a seat on the tube in rush hour.

I don't watch the safety demonstration. I figure if the shit hits the fan, then I'll improvise. Obviously, I'm wearing my seatbelt, the life jacket is under my seat and I don't have a kid to put an oxygen mask on after I secure my own. Sorted. What are the chances of surviving a plane crash anyway?

The plane picks up speed and the cabin is filled with the roar of the engine. My senses are on fire and I can feel my amygdala furiously scanning every inch of the environment. We leave the ground smoothly and surge towards the sky. People excitedly gaze out of the windows, while I look straight ahead. *Oh god, here we go.* For some reason I have the Oasis song 'Supersonic' playing in my head and I cling to the lyrics aggressively, reciting them mentally.

The plane levels after a few minutes, but then dips sharply, making the cabin jolt. *Fuck!* I grit my teeth and feel irrationally angry.

What is wrong with this pilot? Keep the plane straight! Bumps and jerks are not something I even notice when travelling at 125mph to London via train, they don't concern me. I'll happily walk through carriages and risk collapsing into a passenger's lap. Yet, on a plane, I'm in sync with every sound and vibration.

It's not the reality of plummeting to my death that distressing me, it's the knowledge that I'm trapped. David Carbonell confirms that this is in fact common: 'People assume that a flying phobia is all about the fear of crashing. However, the majority of fearful fliers aren't concerned about a crash. They're worried they'll have a panic attack, experience a bout of claustrophobia on the plane, and lose control of themselves somehow.' Claustrophobia is not something I encounter very often, but the thought of being stuck in an endless panic cycle while confined to a small area is devastating. Even after the seatbelt sign has been switched off it's recommended that passengers remain in their seats. I can't pace around if I need to, or move to another location, I must remain in the space assigned to me.

I had a similar experience as we were driving back from London, the previous Christmas. Normally, car journeys don't bother me, but I felt car sick and it dawned on me that for the next four hours I was trapped in a single space. This triggered a cycle of panic that left me feeling desperate. *What if you vomit, or worse? We're nowhere near home.* Dan was driving and my instinct was to beg him to stop at every available service station, but I knew this would make getting back in the car each time that much harder. So I spent most of the journey with my head over a plastic bag, listening to podcasts and reminding myself that we were 'one mile closer'.

Writer Lauren Juliff used to live with a crippling fear of flying. 'Is there anything more embarrassing than being a travel writer with a fear of flying?' she writes. 'I'd have panic attacks, spending many of my flights hyperventilating and crying behind sunglasses. I'd whimper and sob and mutter about how I needed to get off the plane, and every time we safely landed, I'd resolve to never take another flight again.'[3]

That desire to get off the plane, or never get on a plane again, all links back to control. As a teenager, after a flight that featured heavy turbulence, I informed my parents that they had better find another mode of transport to get me home from a holiday in Tenerife, because there was no way I was boarding the flight back. Their lack of interest as they hustled me into a taxi said it all, and yes, of course I flew back. Although I did spend half the flight sitting on my dad's lap while he tried to watch *The Manchurian Candidate* on the shitty TV hanging above us in the aisle.

An obsession with control, as I'm sure you've clocked by now, applies to numerous parts of my life in varying degrees, but the more extremes include: flying, the length of my fringe (only fellow fringe owners will understand this), accidentally letting a murderer in the house (always ask to see ID) and open water. Being uncomfortable with open water makes sense from a primitive perspective. In open water we're at a disadvantage, we can't see what's beneath us and we can't escape as quickly as we could on land. Then there's the possibility that we could get caught in a rip tide and drown. And sharks, let's not forget about sharks.

According to the International Wildlife Museum, the odds of being attacked and killed by a shark are 1 in 3,748,067, with between seventy to a hundred shark attacks worldwide every year. A reassuring statistic when the odds of being killed by a vending machine is higher. Nevertheless, I won't go any deeper into the sea (if I go in at all) than waist height, because despite the evidence, I *will* be the one who gets picked off by a Great White near a Spanish holiday resort. I don't even like being the only one in a swimming pool!

Still, at least in open water I retain some control over the situation; I can, after all, attempt to swim away. Furthermore, it's something that I can avoid all together if I choose to.

Thirty-five thousand feet in the air en route to Philadelphia, I'm once again reminded that I have absolutely no power over my surroundings and there's nothing I can do about it. *You're stuck here for nine hours. NINE HOURS. The air pressure will drop, and you'll struggle to breathe. Can you cope with that?* My eyes burn, but no tears come.

I try to centre myself with deep, belly breathing and remember the advice that Dr Soph gave me. 'Deep breathing sends a message to the brain that everything is OK and that the fight-or-flight response can switch off now.' Simple, but accurate. Belly breathing (literally what it sounds like) is a powerful trick to have in the bag if you experience panic attacks. I found out how to belly breathe from the anxiety coach himself, Dr Carbonell. It works like this:

1. Slump your shoulders and let your body go limp (or as limp as you can).
2. Then exhale as hard as you can. Imagine that you've been told off for something that wasn't your fault, and sigh loudly through your mouth. (Dr Carbonell explains why this is a VERY important step: 'before you can take a deep breath, you have to give one away'.[4] To take a satisfying deep breath you must first clear the lungs of carbon dioxide and make room for the additional oxygen. Hyperventilation occurs when we take lots of shallow breaths, which never satisfy.)

3. Slowly sit up straight, place a hand on your stomach, breathe in through your nose, and as you do so push your stomach out as far as you can.

4. Hold it there for five seconds.

5. Then breathe out through your mouth, sucking the stomach back in.

6. Repeat three times.

You can also watch the 'Breathing Exercises for Panic Attacks, Anxiety & Stress' video on my YouTube channel if you'd prefer a visual demonstration.[5]

Before I knew about laughter yoga, belly breathing was my go-to technique when trying to ease the symptoms of panic. It's not instant, but it does work. Not only does it help to regulate the breathing, but it eases that tightness in the chest muscles.

The whole process of flying really fucks with my rational brain, shaking it off balance. As I mentioned, I find that I'm more emotional when I fly. Travel writer Eli Orzessek wrote an interesting piece about this: 'A study commissioned by Virgin Atlantic in 2011 found that: "over half of respondents (55 per cent) agreed their emotions become heightened when on a flight and 41 per cent of men surveyed said they hid under blankets to hide their tears. As someone who once found himself intensely affected by the Lindsay Lohan classic *Freaky Friday* while on Qatar Airway's epic seventeen-hour flight from Auckland to Doha, I can certainly relate to these statistics."[6]

Dan had a similar experience watching *Zootopia* on our honeymoon. From the waterfall cascading down his face, I presumed he was watching something equivalent to *Schindler's List*, not a story that centred around a young bunny striving to become a cop in an unfair world.

I took a sip of my pint of red wine (no joke, Philadelphians don't piss about with measures), served to me by the flight attendant. It didn't steady me as I'd hoped. I thought it might act as an emotional lubricant and I would find a release in crying. But it doesn't and I feel dehydrated instead. I'd like to say that upon this realisation I discarded the wine, but I didn't; I drank the entire pint and enjoyed the blunted edges of fear for an hour.

In his article, Orzessek quotes Dr Jodi De Luca, a licensed clinical psychologist and expert on altitude and emotions, who is passionate about the impact flying has on the psyche. She argues that everything about standard class travel is inflammatory. The cramped seating arrangements encroach on our physical boundaries. Dan is six foot one and needs an aisle seat if he has any hope of flying comfortably. We both get irrationally angry at people who put their seats back as soon as the seatbelt sign goes off. *Great. I've now lost 25 per cent of my space, which I can't regain without also putting my seat back, which I'd rather not do.* Cabin pressure also plays a role. I'd always struggled with the effects of this and it turns out I'm not alone.

In the same article, Dr Robert Quigley, Medical Director of MedAire, highlights, 'the evidence indicates that we go into a relative state of hypoxia, or oxygen deficiency, during a flight'. In simple terms, the brain is starved of oxygen and we act weird. Some people will cry, others will get angry and some will just fall asleep.

Then there's the attack on the immune system. With an aeroplane's enclosed space, recycled air and passengers travelling when ill, many people complain of feeling unwell after a flight. The pressure of transporting thousands of passengers a day can leave cabin crew unable to clean thoroughly, resulting in tray tables that are 'more germ-ridden than toilets'. As Katherine Harmon, Director of Health Intelligence at the risk-management company IJet, states: 'busy cabin crew may just pick up rubbish, without disinfecting surfaces'.[7] Does anyone else feel sick? A potential attack on the immune system puts the amygdala on high alert.

After years of experiencing panic, I know that preparation is key before going into any potentially triggering environments. I can't just turn up and hope for the best – this never works. I'm far less likely to have a panic attack if I assume that I'm going to have one and put coping strategies in place.

When I'm travelling in any capacity it's all about comfort and protecting the key senses: smell, hearing and sight. I take an aromatherapy oil that I can rub into a scarf and on the top that I'm wearing. I can then inhale this if the air gets stale or a stag party is travelling on board. I like jasmine for its relaxation benefits (but mainly because I just really like the smell!) but a friend of mine swears by peppermint, as it keeps her head clear and prevents travel sickness. Then there's the argument to use tea tree oil due to its antibacterial properties, but to be honest, I just rub hand sanitiser around my nose for that!

I have a super padded cosy eye mask that also acts as a cushion. This keeps out that piercing aeroplane lighting if I'm trying to sleep or pretend I'm somewhere else. I also have huge headphones to keep the harsh sound of the engine from distracting me. Noise is a big one for me. A therapist once even suggested that from a sensory perspective, I might be on the autistic spectrum. I have a highly emotional response to unpleasant sounds: the washing machine for example, lawnmowers, people sniffing, or the brakes of the tube as it pulls into the station. Even groups of people interacting loudly in bars can set me off. The official term for this is misophonia (selective sound sensitivity syndrome).

So, with my oil and scarf, eye mask and headphones, I had my senses covered. Then there was comfy clothing and my inflight beauty routine. (Thank you Lisa Eldridge for teaching me this via your YouTube channel.[8]) Basically, I give myself a facial, using micellar water, cotton pads, a (clear) face mask, hydrating serum and moisturiser. It's a pleasant activity and great distraction. I have a book and two films downloaded on my phone, in case I can't watch films on the flight.

Even with considerable preparation, there's still no guarantee that panic won't rear its head, and true to form, sixty minutes into the flight, *IT* hit. The main event.

The seatbelt sign flashed on and the captain announced that we'd shortly experience some 'moderate turbulence'. Moderate? Lying bastard. It felt like a giant toddler was using the plane as a saltshaker! I buried my head in my hands and tried not to hyperventilate. *I can't breathe. I can't cope. I don't want this. I can't bear the thought of feeling this bad for the next eight hours.* I was falling, as though I didn't have control of my body and I struggled to move my arms. I was in a state of hyper-fear and it consumed me.

What about the Oblivion approach? The thought pops into my head out of nowhere. As the plane jolted and dipped, an experience that I'd had aged seventeen came back to me. I went to Alton Towers with some friends and a boy who I really fancied at the time. To clarify, big rides scared the shit out of me (surprise, surprise), and while I could bypass a few, there were some I couldn't get out of without seeming boring. This, sadly, included Oblivion. (For those unfamiliar with Oblivion, it's a well-known British fairground ride that consists of one, huge, vertical drop.) I spent forty-five minutes in the queue, laughing and pretending to be fine, but secretly hoping to spontaneously combust. Or if the ride could (safely) break down, that'd be wonderful.

Although I didn't understand it at the time, my amygdala felt threatened: it feared that this ride would kill me somehow and activated the fight-or-flight response.

Before I knew it, we were being ushered into an available car. *Oh my god, you're actually doing this, this is actually going to happen.* My entire body turned to jelly, and a member of staff had to help me fasten my seatbelt, due to my clumsy, trembling hands. I was practically high on terror. Speechless.

Yet, as the ride started a thought occurred to me: *This whole thing is bigger than you, and there is literally NOTHING that you can do about it now. Just lean in and observe. Let go.*

A warm surge of calm energy came over me, that I didn't expect. Rather than trying to control the fear, or battle with it, I gave in to the situation entirely. I realised then that it didn't matter how much I worried, or how hysterical I became, nothing would stop the carriage from moving along the tracks, edging closer to the drop. The whole thing was inevitable. So ... fuck it. Once I'd made the 'fuck it' decision, I felt numb, tingly even. The iron grip of terror that only moments earlier was choking the life out of me, loosened and became quiet. *Fuck it,* I muttered once more as we went over the edge and into the darkness.

I didn't enjoy the ride per se, but it also didn't devastate me mentally, though the same cannot be said for the boy I fancied. He went on to become my first proper boyfriend. Over a four-year period, he cheated on me numerous times and I always randomly found out via Facebook, when some disgruntled partner would DM me. Although brutal, at least the Oblivion trauma was over quickly!

In his book *Happy*, Derren Brown touches on humanity's fear of death (or oblivion), which is inevitable and therefore pointless. It cannot be avoided and the fear of it is therefore a waste of energy, or mental space. Referencing the philosopher Epicurus, he says: 'So, death, the most terrifying of ills, is nothing to us, since so long as we exist, death is not with us. It does not concern either the living or the dead.'[9]

Basically, when death comes, we won't be around to experience it. So why bother obsessing?

I took this attitude with the Oblivion ride. Once it had set off there was nothing I could do. The ride would complete the track whether I worried or not. Life continues whether I worry or not.

I don't know why this revelation came back to me after fifteen years. Maybe it was my work with 'accepting' a panic attack, but in the grips of a monstrous attack I suddenly thought of Oblivion. *There's nothing you can do. If the plane is going to crash, then it's going to crash. You're stuck in this seat with fear and there is nothing you can do. So, let's welcome the sensation, let IT take the reins for a while, as we nod politely. We know how to deal with trash talk and we know about the panic trick. So, fuck it, let go.*

There's a certain euphoria that comes with letting go of the reins.

It wasn't my job to try and 'stop' the panic attack on that flight, or to control it in any way, all I had to do was sit back and simply let the time pass. So that's exactly what I did, I sat back and let panic wash over me with zero resistance or distraction for a good ten minutes. I allowed fear, terror, discomfort and rage to circulate with force. In many ways I'd learned that the 'threat' of panic was far worse than the attack itself. 'When you anticipate, you're free to imagine any kind of danger, no matter how unrealistic.'[10] Reality in contrast is more restrictive and our thoughts are limited to circumstance. Basically, the longer you spend in a situation that frightens you, the sooner you'll realise that you've been tricked by panic. Thoughts are a symptom of panic and they trigger an emotional response.

On the flight there was something liberating about 'letting it out'. I felt detached from the situation, as though I was a researcher observing a condition, rather than experiencing it myself. As the plane jerked back and forth, I just sat there. Panic raged with a variety of symptoms, but I did nothing.

You can't bully me any more, I thought. *You'll flare up no matter what I do, no matter how much I prepare, or what techniques I deploy. So, fuck it. I don't care any more.*

That turned out to be the best flight I'd ever had, to the point that I actually enjoyed myself. I watched films, did some reading and even slept a little. Normal things, that many people take for granted. The notion that 'it doesn't matter what I do, I have no control' liberated me.

The internal conversation went something like this:

What if we have another attack?
Then we'll have another attack
But what if it's worse?
Then it's worse.
What if it doesn't end?
Not my problem, it'll end when it ends.

I found a genuine sense of peace in being completely passive.

*

During the flight back I didn't experience a single attack. I was confident in my pre-planned response should anything happen, but it wasn't needed. Turns out that acceptance is more powerful than even a pint of wine!

CHAPTER 8

Act Normal: Dating, Relationships and the Relationship You Have with Yourself

D an knew from the beginning that there was something a little, well … 'off centre' about me, as he politely puts it. Being a serial dater by the time our paths crossed, he was a lot more experienced than I was and had developed a sort of first-date 'routine', which I promptly destroyed by not complying in any way. For example, on our first date he went in for a friendly hug as a greeting, whereas I firmly stuck my hand out for him to shake and blurted: 'You're not a murderer, are you?' (The logic being that all murderers must identify themselves when asked.) This point-blank approach and 'odd' questioning is another reason why a previous shrink suggested that I'd been born on the spectrum, but that this went undiagnosed (as it does with a lot of girls) because school taught me how to 'behave appropriately' in social situations. 'Over the years, the strain of the school environment triggered the onset on social anxiety.' (Her words not mine.) I'm not sure about this theory myself; I think I just behave strangely when I'm nervous or uncomfortable.

Still, I take her point considering the first thing that I ever said to her was: 'I don't like this, I don't want to be here, and your jumper is distracting me.' Then refused to sit down.

Dan and I officially met on a dating app, and after the awkward face-to-face introduction, we went to a nearby pub. I then proceeded to down an entire glass of wine the moment his head was turned. (My hands were practically vibrating with nerves. A hefty glug was the only option to take the edge off, other than doing twenty star jumps on the spot, which for the record, I have done on previous occasions.) Downing 175ml of Sauvignon Blanc in under ten seconds is no laughing matter. It's very unpleasant (because I prefer Chardonnay).

During this period of my life, I was living in the grips of social anxiety, which hadn't yet been diagnosed. This would explain some of my 'interesting' behaviour during the first year of our courtship. In no particular order:

- Legging it in the opposite direction if I saw him in public.
- Freezing in horror if he spontaneously changed plans. Particularly if it involved other people or arriving earlier than planned.
- Grinning manically to try and hide said horror. Dan calls this my 'Cheshire Cat' face. My rationale being if I just kept smiling, then nobody would notice that my head was about to explode.
- Asking him NOT to look at me, randomly and without explanation. (I find direct eye contact really intense sometimes.)
- Leaving a party ten minutes after we arrived.
- Locking myself in our hotel bathroom for over an hour on our first holiday together. (Long story.)

Magical. Distorted rom-com material.

I suppose I'd always taken what might be labelled a 'unique' approach to finding a mate. For example, it's a sure bet that I fancy a person if I ignore them face to face and correspond exclusively via message (text, MSN, WhatsApp or whatever). Cute behaviour for a teenager, not so much an adult.

If we make it as far as a date, then you can expect me to be what my husband calls 'aggy' for the first twenty to thirty minutes. I tease, joke, ask all the questions and deflect any that come my way. Classic 'defence behaviour', I'd go on the attack before anyone has the chance to expose my vulnerabilities. Again, all fairly standard fight-or-flight responses upon reflection. I was anxious, which my amygdala wrongly identified as danger and jumped into action.

If (and only if) the person successfully tolerated my company for an hour, then traces of my real personality would creep out. My amygdala – satisfied that I wasn't in peril – would go back to sleep and let the rational part of my brain come out to play.

I'll admit, it's an unusual approach. But one that has, in my defence, had a solid success rate. I've only been in two relationships in my life. The first lasted four years and I married the second! (Watch this space for my next book on eccentric courting techniques.)

It's easy to look back with hindsight and think, *Oh fuck, THAT's what that was, all is explained and therefore forgiven*. Yet, the way I behaved when dating really does make me cringe. As a well-rounded and stable adult, I recognise that by trying to suppress my feelings of discomfort, rather than work with them, I was making the symptoms of anxiety worse. As a young woman in her early twenties, suppression seemed like an excellent idea! The only idea even.

It makes sense that I'd find a standard 'date' triggering. They are too 'set' and formal and feel almost like a performance by both participants. I reckon I would've been more comfortable if I was blindsided by a less conventional date, somewhere random and low-key. Less time for my anxious brain to latch on to the situation.

The truth is, I was afraid that if Dan saw the real me, then he might leave. So, I tried my best to shield him from my anxiety and if I could have shielded him from panic too, then I would have.

Unfortunately, panic doesn't tolerate that shit and it burst from my subconscious like a freight train, knocking us both down in the process.

The fear of scaring someone off is common. 'Crazy' or not, no one likes the idea of a potential 'love interest' seeing our negative traits too early on in the relationship. Dan's equivalent of this, for example, was pretending to enjoy staying out past 9 p.m. on a work night, something that still makes him shudder. 'I was exhausted during that period,' he told me. 'It would get to ten o'clock and I'd panic; by the time I got home it'd be eleven! That's barbaric! I knew that I just needed to hook you in with my amazing personality, before revealing that I'm actually incredibly boring.'

Crazy and boring, not a bad combo as it turns out.

Common dating fears for people who experience panic attacks are as follows:

- What if they think I'm a freak/loser?
- How will I explain what's happening if I have an attack?
- What if I have sweat patches/start blushing/start shaking?
- What if I lose control and do something weird?
- What if they leave after five minutes?

Anna, a 27-year-old hairdresser from Essex, talks to me about her panic attack fears when dating:

It's as though I'm stuck in a prison of my own making. It's fine when we're talking on the phone or messaging, but face to face is a nightmare. I spend the whole time on edge just waiting for *IT* to happen. On one date I said that I was going to the bar and just left. How could I tell him what was going on? I must've looked mental. The poor bloke tried to message me afterwards, but I was too embarrassed to reply. It's like I don't have control of my body, I'm a slave to panic attacks.

Ryan, an assistant architect from Oxford, tells me:

Sometimes I get away with it, especially if I have a few drinks, but I'm always expecting the worse. The gay community is overtly confident in a stereotypical sense, and I feel like a loser for being so shy. My current partner finds my blushing 'cute', but I hate that panic has such an obvious hold over me. I've lost count of the number of dates I've cancelled over the years because I can't cope with the dread that I might have a panic attack. I can't stand the thought that someone might notice.

Natalie, a student from Bolton, says:

It's the 'pre-date panic' that I struggle with the most. I've cancelled so many dates because a panic attack stopped me from physically leaving the flat. The symptoms would start hours in advance. I'd be sweating through my clothes and feel breathless and dizzy. Once it was so bad, I couldn't get up off the floor for an hour. I postponed the meeting time and then eventually cancelled. What would they think of me? How would I explain my weird behaviour? 'Hi! My name's Natalie and I'm a nervous wreck. Is that sexy to you?'

I reasoned that, if I felt this bad now, imagine how much worse it'd be once I arrived.

Leah, a writer from Los Angeles, goes into more detail:

I have had a tough time with dates for the last six years because my anxiety kicks into high gear in restaurants. One that vividly comes to mind was on my twenty-sixth birthday. I went out to my favourite restaurant with a guy I'd been dating and even though I was really excited for the night, I had this pit in my stomach even before I met up with him. We sit down and the first thing I notice is that my neck and chest feel so stiff and tight that I can't concentrate on anything else. I'm looking at him and trying to make conversation and he's coming in and out of focus. Normally I would just tell someone I am feeling panicky or weird because I've made a point about being more open about it, but I really wanted to have one night out where I wasn't the anxious girl who couldn't handle a crowd and the obligation to sit down until a meal was over. The food probably came out pretty quickly, but it felt like an eternity and I kept checking the clock every thirty seconds to see if it was almost time to leave. Normally I use people I'm with as kind of an anchor when I feel like I'm flying off into a panic attack, but it is so much harder to admit to myself and other people that I'm having a hard time when I want moments to be special. I rushed through the night and then made an excuse to leave and cry. It felt awful!

Restaurants are a known trigger of panic attacks, one that I've experienced myself. As a condition, it's known as deipnophobia, 'A fear of banquets or dinner parties' (bloody banquets causing trouble again). The noise, the closed space, the unspoken formality, and the knowledge that you must remain seated and behave 'normally' for the duration.

Dating is hard enough without adding panic to the mix. The idea is to have fun and focus on witty banter, not worrying about accessing the emergency exits, or which item on the menu will be the easiest to swallow if your throat seizes up. I've never had this symptom personally, but it's common enough. (Definitely go for soup.)

We want to be appealing on those precious first interactions and for many people, that includes appearing to be easy-going. Unfortunately, this pressure has the potential to make anxiety and panic worse.

During that year, I researched some of the dating advice given by popular women's magazine *Glamour*:

'Give him direct eye contact, about 80 per cent of the conversation, be positive, and smile easily,' says dateologist Tracy Steinberg. 'A group of wild coyotes could break down the door, but you would be too enthralled to notice!'

I mean my amygdala would DEFINITELY notice Tracy. I expect I'd be the first one out of there ... Also, how the fuck do I calculate the 80 per cent? I might get it wrong and end up staring aggressively for an hour!

'Humans have evolved to read the emotions of others, and one way we do it is by looking into the eyes. When we touch each other, even with a casual arm stroke or a friendly hug, and look into each other's eyes, we can trigger a series of chemical events in the brain that lead us to open ourselves up to another person. A hormone called oxytocin is released, driving this response. That's followed by dopamine, a chemical that motivates us to seek out rewarding experiences.'[1]

That seems like a lot of pressure to me. Can't we just have a few drinks, or go for a walk in the park?

During my twenties, magazine articles encouraged women to appear fun, easy-going and, where possible, be tanned with big tits.

This would certainly explain why I agreed to play crazy golf with Steven Davis at the Trafford Centre back in 2010. Two layers of fake tan rested on the surface of my skin and a push-up bra forced my breasts to be more impressive. What a first and last date that was. For starters I hate golf and I'm completely hopeless at it. Whereas he took the 'sport' very seriously and by the sixth hole angrily demanded that I 'commit to a shot'! It was hard to take his rage seriously on account of the golf course being dinosaur-themed. I hated every-thing about that date, from the golf, the burger joint afterwards and the car journey home, in which he blasted heavy metal from the stereo. Each time I felt the urge to shout: 'Can you turn this shit off, please?' I'd look at his beautiful face (he really was fit) and decide not to make a fuss. Are beautiful people aware of their power, or do they just take it for granted, I wonder?

Back home, I spent the rest of the evening feeling wired and on edge. I'd agreed to a date that I knew would stress me out and I spent the remainder of the evening dealing with the consequences. Worse

still, rather than being easy on myself, I berated myself for not finding it fun.

I can't say that I learned my lesson by the time I met Dan, as our
courtship will tell, but then where's the fun in learning life's lessons
before the age of thirty anyway? I agreed to meet his friends spontaneously on our fifth date, after a trip to the Natural History Museum.
'They're just at the pub around the corner if you fancy it?' My heart
was pounding, and I wanted to scream, but I said 'yes' with a smile.
Sitting in a crowded, loud area with seven (perfectly nice) people I'd
never met before was uncomfortable. I spent the entire time agitated
and feeling 'under threat'.

We'd been together nine months when I had my nervous breakdown. After the infamous 'Jane Austen' aborted interview that day,
I tried to hide what had happened from him when he came home
from work. *You've managed to trick this man into moving in with you.*
If he sees who you really are now, he'll leave. However, unlike anxiety,
panic will not be silenced or repressed, and it doesn't give a shit
about who sees it.

Turns out that Dan could deal with my condition – I'd just never
given him the chance. It also turns out that his love is unconditional.

Self-love

'Would you talk to a friend the way that you talk to yourself?'

I don't think anything infuriates me more than this phrase and
it's one I've heard multiple times over the years. The patronising
simplicity of it really grates, because of course the answer is 'no'. Yet
it misses the point entirely. *I wouldn't talk to a friend that way because*

I care about my friend; they deserve love and respect whereas I don't.
Herein lies the problem.

People who live with mental illness tend to have a warped view of themselves and – surprise, surprise – it's usually negative.

The very idea of self-love during this stage of my life was repulsive. I preferred instead not to think about it at all and just plod along.

'Everybody is self-critical,' an old colleague once quipped, rolling her eyes. 'It's not just unique to you, Claire!'

Another roadblock I've encountered when talking about mental illness is the determination of some people to point out that everyone deals with the same 'niggles' you do, thereby making your focus on it self-indulgent. It's tricky to get around without being confrontational. *Does your inner critic tell you to slam your fingers in a drawer when you make a mistake, Joanna? No? Well fuck off then.*

Another standard one is: 'Everyone feels nervous before doing X' or 'You're just a little shy.'

It's not that I disagree with this; it's true, everyone feels nervous or shy at times, and everyone has a self-critical internal dialogue.

It's difficult to articulate when a person lacks a frame of reference. They haven't experienced it, so they don't understand how bad it can get. Which is true of all conditions, whether mental or physical. I don't know how it feels to have arthritis, for example, but then I also don't offer my opinion on what I 'think' it feels like.

It's hard to have compassion towards yourself, when society objects to it, as though everyone is experiencing the same thing and you're just weaker than most. Or as Amanda, a long-time follower of my blog, tells me: 'Self-love? You're joking. I'd first have to convince my family that I'm not just a "worrier", I have panic attacks.

We tell the kids that "mummy is just being silly" when I'm crying because I can't catch my breath. The narrative is all wrong. It makes me feel worthless and afterwards I hate myself.'

Even years into my recovery, my relationship with myself was cruel at best and abusive at worst. It was something that just wouldn't shift, like all habits that have been deeply ingrained.

The worst remits of control were focused on my personal image. How I wanted to be seen and how I wanted others to see me. As I mentioned in chapter 2, I was still very much living in a warped version of the world where love was conditional and had to be earned via the 'correct behaviour'. Incorrect behaviour would result in love and kinship being withheld. I learned this (inaccurately) from a young age and clung to it. There were desirable character traits and undesirable ones, according to whoever was talking at the time – teachers, family, friends, friends' parents, employers, colleagues.

I have a weird skill and it's hard to write about. Basically, give me ten minutes in anyone's company and I can figure out in detail what personality traits they like (sometimes I can do it in five). Then it's simple, I just become *that* person for the duration. I don't always crack it, but I'm decent. We all do it to an extent; part of social interaction is seeking to integrate by finding common ground. I just took it to the extreme, sort of like a deranged game.

The obvious problem with this approach is that as we go through life, desirable traits change, and I found myself altering my personality constantly both in my professional and personal life. 'Achieving' someone's favour, as in 'making them like me' became the ultimate thrill. I was good at it, and it became an addiction.

Reading this now, the whole thing strikes a tragic tone, but it didn't feel that way at the time. I enjoyed pretending to be someone else because it allowed me to escape my mind for a bit. A way to focus all of that excess mental energy. And I'd be lying if I said I was completely over the habit. It comes in handy when I'm trying to blag something or get myself out of trouble!

I spent a large portion of my life crippled by self-loathing, and I attached my self-worth largely to what others thought of me. So, it's fortunate that I ended up with such a kind and encouraging man. Not to mention patient. I tried very hard to push him away after my break-down, mortified by the version of me that he'd witnessed. The screaming, crying, out-of-control Claire who begged for help and crawled about on the floor. How would he ever see me as anything else? How would I ever see me as anything else when I looked at him? To cut a long story short, it didn't work. He wasn't having any of it. 'Panic tricked you into believing that you behaved more recklessly than you actually did,' David Carbonell tells me at a later date. It turns out that my behaviour was barely interesting, let alone disruptive! 'You cried a lot and rang a hotline, so maybe give yourself a break.'

'How about you tell me how you're feeling and what *you* want to do for a change?' Dan asks when I come back to our flat after a month-long absence.

'Honestly? I want to play top trumps and eat a Twirl.'

Sorted. That was our evening.

It took me a while, but I realised that over a twenty-year period self-repression had become a habit. One that I'd never tried to alter. It was an addiction, and like all addictions it clouded my judgement, tainted my dating history, my personal life and my relationship with myself. I couldn't have a positive and loving relationship with 'me' because I didn't know how. It hadn't existed as a priority until this point.

Changing this habit wasn't easy, and I struggled to relate to many of the approaches that claimed to help. 'Write a list of things to be thankful for every morning'. *Every morning? Seriously?* 'Shout out positive affirmations to the universe!' *Oh, fuck off.*

As with many things, in the end I found my niche by accident. I met an incredible lady at a fundraiser and googled her afterwards. It turns out that this lady was Shahroo Izadi, author of *The Kindness Method*. Now if that ain't fate, then I don't know what is! I learned a great deal from her 'visual-mapping' techniques, centred around honesty and a no-nonsense approach. I respond well to physical evidence that I can see. Shahroo advises readers to create 'maps' to refer back to when they're struggling. For example, 'In the centre of a piece of paper write "things that I'm proud of" and draw a bubble around it.'[2] I was sceptical about the impact, but on days when I feel abusive, I look at that map and it helps me to challenge the negative thoughts that come so naturally. After a panic attack, for example, I struggle to remember anything good about me, so it's useful to have a pre-written reminder that I can refer to. I have a map that highlights how many symptoms of panic I have survived and I also have a map of 'things I like' and 'things I don't like'. These maps in particular have prevented me from agreeing to events 'off the cuff' just to please someone else.

Email: We'd love you to travel to Cumbria and do a talk on the dangers of social media, then have dinner with the faculty afterwards.

Instinct: Just say yes, you don't want to piss them off, it might stop you from getting other work.

Rational brain: According to your maps, you don't like public speaking, nor do you like long uncomfortable train journeys and dining with academics who make you feel pressured to seem 'smart'. You can say no, you're allowed to say no.

This new-found self-respect had a huge impact on how I relate to others. I'm my actual self when I meet people now, which is huge! It still makes me feel vulnerable, but I've made peace with that. Not everyone in life has to like me (although I do have to remind myself of this). The silver lining is that I can spot earlier those people I don't want in my life, rather than discovering this months later. Honesty really does just make things easier!

I spoke to my friend, mental health consultant Ruth Cooper-Dickson about this. She takes a very up-front approach when meeting new people, even in the early stages of dating. Recently, she experienced a panic attack on a first date and dealt with it openly. 'We were on the tube chatting away, and then I felt *IT*. Like a wave of heat. I turned scarlet and moved towards the window in between carriages. I was conscious of his worried and confused glances, but I didn't want to hide it from him. I've wasted enough time feeling ashamed.'

She dived straight in at the deep end and explained what was happening. She was practical, but direct. As her mental health is a key aspect of who she is, it's not something she's willing to hide. This honesty is her gift to her brain. A true act of self-love. It also enables her to spot people who are 'keepers' and those who are not worth her time.

Being honest is awkward, but necessary, and I'm not ashamed. I like to tell dates in advance, rather than 'put them on the spot'. Just a simple message such as: 'Occasionally I experience panic attacks. If it happens on our date please don't worry, I'll be fine in a few moments, I just have to go for a walk and wait for it to pass. Looking forward to hanging out later!' For me, it's about owning my panic and taking steps to help me feel more comfortable.

– **Priya**

Can you imagine how different things might have been if I'd just told Steven Davis, 'I think I'd be really self-conscious playing golf on a first date and I'd rather be relaxed. Maybe on the next one? *wink* Any chance we can just do something low-key, like a coffee?'

I expect the outcome would have remained the same, largely because of personality differences and his lack of humour (because obviously I'm hilarious).

This was a hard chapter to write because it's taken me a long time to build the foundations of self-love. Still, self-respect – if not love – has become an integral part of my panic rehabilitation. It's weird to admit that you're not used to being yourself, but I'm getting there.

What I should have said to Dan when we initially moved in together is:

'I'm fucking crazy, OK. I freak out about oxygen levels, I'm convinced I'm going to be murdered, I don't like sitting across from people until I know them, and I can't do "normal" small talk without practice. I'm not bubbly, meeting new people stresses me out, I hate all sports, especially football, and I talk a lot of shit. At some point in our relationship you will need to escort me to the toilet if I've had a nightmare and then play Jenga to calm me down. On the plus side, I have long legs, I'm very loyal and I PROMISE that you'll never be bored.'

CHAPTER 9

Learning to Talk About Panic

It's 11 a.m. and I'm in Eastbourne for work, having a meeting with a junior book buyer called Ellie. Eastbourne is a deceptively long journey from London, which I find out moments after the train departs. Sitting cosy with my hot chocolate in the carriage, I expect the train manager to announce a forty-minute jaunt, not two hours. *Bollocks*.

The meeting room I find myself in is nothing special. It's grey and devoid of any character, with the exception of a signed photo of Delia Smith and a Gruffalo poster on the wall. I find this oddly calming rather than depressing. Nothing unnerves me quite like a giant, trendy meeting space. The type with marble tables and lush carpet on the floors. Maybe a few canvas paintings dotted about like motivational titbits. 'Think like there is no box!' Or 'I'm not here to be average, I'm here to be awesome!'

In one such office I visited, there was even a swing in the corner, and yes of course I had a go. Who in their right mind is immune to swing fun? Or a slide for that matter. Although I do draw the line at ball pools.

Ellie offers me a hot drink, and even though I'd prefer water, I accept. It's bad manners to refuse a hot drink where I'm from, no matter the weather. 'Scalding hot tea in the desert? I'd love one yeah, cheers.' She returns five minutes later, and I notice that her hands are shaking. Tea spills over the rim of the mug as she places it on the table. 'Oh, sorry!' she mumbles, obviously embarrassed. The flush of her cheeks spreads to her ears and chest.

'That's all right,' I say, 'I can't carry more than one cup either!'

I don't think she hears my response; still, I take out my notes and wait for her to start. She lifts her cup to her mouth, but then slams it down on the table without even taking a sip. I pretend not to notice her now-crimson cheeks, hopeful that she'll relax if we chat about non-work-related things for a few minutes. Saying that, small talk isn't exactly my speciality and I resist the urge to talk about the weather. Instead I ask about Eastbourne: 'My train back isn't until later this afternoon, is there anywhere nice I should have a wander?' She can't meet my eye and my spider senses are starting to tingle. 'Excuse me a second!' she snaps, knocking her chair over as she darts out of the room. *Is this avoidance?* I think. *Am I witnessing avoidance?* I'm not a shrink, but I recognise frantic behaviour when I see it.

It takes ten minutes for her to return this time and she makes a point of over-explaining her absence. It sounds stale, rehearsed even; something I'd done myself many times.

What the fuck do I do here? She's clearly having a bad one.

'Shall I tell you about some of our summer books?' I smile, hoping that by taking charge I can distract her. She looks up, finally meeting my eye and that's when I see *IT*, the fear that's beginning to take hold. Her whole body is now visibly trembling, and tears are pooling at the rims of her eyes. She shakes her head rapidly and the roller coaster I've come to know so well begins, except this time I'm an observer.

'I can't, I can't,' she whispers, so quietly I have to lip-read.

I practically launch myself across the table and take both of her hands in mine. 'It's OK,' I say with as much calm authority as I can muster. 'You're OK.'

'I can't breathe! Oh god, I'm so sorry!' She jerks back and tries to stand up, but I keep hold of her hands. I know what she wants to do, what her brain is screaming at her to do, but I also know from experience that her brain is 'backfiring', that she needs to sit still a moment longer so that it can stabilise. 'Has this happened before?' I ask. The tears stream down her face as she nods. 'I thought it was a caffeine problem, but I haven't had any today. I don't know what's wrong. Please help me! I'm sorry, I'm so sorry.'

I can see myself reflected in her eyes and it stabs at my heart. The mixture of horror and guilt is dire. I now appreciate what it must be like for those closest to me to witness me in this state. Nobody likes to see another person in distress. 'OK, listen,' I say soothingly with as much authority as I can muster. 'I know exactly what this is, it's a panic attack. I understand that you feel really scared, but I *promise* you that nothing bad is going to happen. You've done nothing wrong and I'm completely cool with all of this. You've done nothing to be ashamed of. We just need to make you more comfortable until it passes.'

She continues shaking her head and tries to stand once more. 'What if someone sees? What will they think!'

My grip on her hand tightens. 'It's fine! Maybe they'll think we've been having an illicit affair, and you're devastated that I'm dumping you for another buyer in the office. One with more money!'

She looks momentarily confused and then laughs. *IT* retreats slightly in the face of humour. I tell her to forget about the meeting, I can just email the rest of the 'new books' information later. *Fuck it*.

We spend the rest of the hour talking about her kitten and my breakdown.

I never really liked the 'you're not alone' slogan that became cemented with mental health campaigns. It felt disingenuous, like a cruel joke at a time in my life when I'd never felt more alien. In my mind, panic had 'selected' me to torture and shame. Everyone else could cope with it quietly and without fuss. Worse, they were thriving. Yet there I was with Ellie, seeing something so familiar in the eyes of a stranger.

A key characteristic of any mental illness is that the sufferer can feel as though they're an anomaly. Despite statistics proving this is not the case and said awareness campaigns, it can be difficult to believe when you're the one going through it. Optimism doesn't help when it's you trying to keep the storm at bay or fight your way off the bathroom floor yet again. I understand that, truly. Pretty words won't keep your head above the waves. So, what will? Or at least make it easier?

The more I work in this field the more I understand how rare it is for people to be direct about their mental health and their own battle with the waves. Instead, they talk in hushed tones, or corner me privately. They send me DMs and emails.

This realisation became even more apparent to me in 2017, when I did a talk at the Disney Expo at their London HQ. I'm still not sure what the Expo stood for exactly, or what the event was about ... but fuck what an amazing office they have, complete with a full-size model of the *Millennium Falcon* (naturally, I climbed on board and had a play). I also had my picture taken with full-size replicas of the Avengers.

How could such a magical office have any problems ... And not pay their speakers? *Cough.*

Everyone was genuinely lovely and the talk itself went very well, with the exception of an IT issue. My laptop wouldn't connect to their fancy projector thing, like not at all, nada, no go. I was starting to freak out, when a man approached me and said: 'Is it Adele? Is it Adele?' To which I replied semi-hysterically: 'NO! MY NAME'S CLAIRE!' He paused and smiled patiently and I realised he was actually from the IT department 'No ... I mean is your laptop a Dell?' I laughed, he laughed. What a legend.

I spoke about the importance of workplace mental health and shared my story as an example or, as I like to call it, a cautionary tale. I had no idea whether it would connect, but barely ten minutes after I'd left the building, I received several emails:

Thank you for talking about panic attacks specifically. I think I have them too. At first, I thought it was anxiety, but based on what you said, panic attacks make more sense. People in my team think I'm quiet, but I really just struggle to speak up in meetings. Every time I try my heart starts pounding, I blush and then feel sweaty and faint. How can I explain this without outing myself as the office weirdo?

My manager wants me to take an internal course on 'giving presentations with confidence', but I keep making excuses to avoid it. Public speaking is my worst nightmare and I know that I'll have a panic attack and humiliate myself. The last time that I presented anything was at university and the only reason I got through that is because I smoked weed. I can't smoke weed at work, and I can't risk having a panic attack. I'm desperate for advice.

The email that intrigued me the most was:

I started having what I think are panic attacks sixth months ago. I was asked a difficult question in a budget meeting and became flustered. Eventually I had to leave the room because I felt dizzy and was having difficulty breathing. It was embarrassing and I felt unprofessional, but I just put the experience down as 'one of those things'. My wife said it might've been because I was hungover that day, so I cut out drinking during the weeknights. However, I keep having these attacks in meetings. I'm in my late thirties now and at management level. This is something that might be acceptable for juniors, but not for me. Talking about emotions is frowned upon and I'm concerned that talking to anyone about this will damage me in some way. I have too much to lose and can't afford a black mark against my name.

These concerns echoed my own. At one time, I observed my working environment and didn't feel safe. Not in a literal sense, of course, but emotionally. The people in my department were extrovert, unflappable and tough. I was enamoured by them, in awe even. Nobody 'stumbled' in meetings or shied away from attention; they were solid.

So how could I be the one to break the chain? The odd one out? It was better to just crack on and ignore the (now) obvious signs of anxiety, hoping that I would get stronger over time. We're told that ultimately experience makes us stronger and I held on to this notion tight.

We learn from our early school years that revealing something quirky about your personality (a love of vintage writing sets, for example) is risky. People don't always react positively, or act in a way that we expected.

My first taste of being judged negatively because of my mental health condition was at secondary school. Undiagnosed at the time, teachers were irritated by how much I worried. I mean I get it, the last thing an overworked teacher needs is a needy kid, stressing about shit that they really don't need to be stressing about. Still, it was considered a 'character flaw', and something that I should be able to control, like untidiness, rather than being accepted as an aspect of my personality. It certainly wasn't identified as a sign of a troubled mind. After numerous dressing-downs from teachers for being 'overly sensitive' and 'daydreaming', I learned to hide this side of myself. It was obviously something to be ashamed of.

With regard to panic attacks, some of the key stigmas and misconceptions include:

- It's just an overreaction to really bad stress
- It's a sign of weakness, a person who can't handle pressure
- It's the sign of a person who cannot control their emotions and is naturally prone to hysteria
- They cannot be helped, and the person must withdraw from all activities that trigger them

With shit like that flying around, is it any wonder that so many keep their personal struggles a secret?

Still, this isn't the early noughties any more, we're now more than two decades into the twenty-first century, and attitudes are changing, albeit slowly. UK schools have progressed greatly and rapidly in both mental health education and providing support for students. Surely, an inspiration to the workplace.

Being open about a personal condition can be difficult, because sticking one's neck on the chopping block is never a pleasant experience. What if nobody joins you? What if you're ostracised? For all the positive campaigning to lessen the stigma of mental illness in recent years, it's still not socially acceptable to admit that you're struggling with mental illness.

Panic, like anxiety, is not considered to be what I heard one person at an education conference call 'a big deal'. She went on to say that it's no more than being a bit 'flustered' or 'stressed', and that 'some people do like to blow things out of proportion'. I winced inwardly – was she talking about me? I had been on stage talking about student mental health ten minutes prior. For someone who'd never experienced a panic attack, she seemed to have an awful lot of opinions about them. I couldn't help but feel disappointed by her attitude, not to mention livid, but what can you do in a room full of 300 delegates? Am I immature enough to 'accidentally' kick her coffee over? Of course I am! Unfortunately, it was just out of reach.

It tends to be people who've never suffered a panic attack who make blanket statements and assumptions. It's easy to write them off as being neurotic, dramatic or attention seeking.

We've reached a time in which mental illness is being categorised in the media, TV and film. Assumptions about the severity of a condition depends on how it's portrayed. While bipolar disorder and depression have arguably been represented successfully, both anxiety and panic still lack adequate portrayal. To date I haven't seen anything that highlights the devastating effects of a panic attack. Instead, TV and films tend to go down the comical route, for example, a 'nerd' hyperventilating into a brown paper bag because an attractive girl spoke to him.

How can we expect things to change if we don't speak out?

My breakdown in 2012 forced me to talk about my mental health, because the 'cat was out of the bag', so to speak. However, I was slow to open up about my experiences with panic, focusing on my recovery instead. But, after witnessing Ellie's attack that day, I decided to take action, or at least have a crack at it. I'd been working with Ellie for months. She was great at her job and clearly had a passion for books. Yet, panic had been slowly chipping away at her mental state, making her feel worthless. Of course, she felt worthless, there was very little information out there to tell her that she wasn't, or even information that explained what her condition was in an accessible way.

I started my blog *We're All Mad Here* for selfish reasons initially. As I mentioned in chapter 3, I find writing very therapeutic, and at the time, it was a great outlet. Think brain vomit coupled with emotional rants. However, a few weeks into my recovery and journey with mental health, I became frustrated with the amount of medical jargon used. How are people supposed to talk about panic if they can't even understand or feel intimidated by the language?

Bear in mind that in 2013, there wasn't as much accessible information available to the public as there is now. So, I went into my GP appointments with a notepad and whenever I didn't understand a word (cortisol, serotonin, amygdala, SSRI, CBT, benzo-diazepines …) I would ask my doctor to explain. I also spent time 'translating' medical journals that I found online. I strongly believe that education is a basic right, not a privilege. Knowledge should be available to everyone and not held hostage by opaque terminology and outdated systems.

Besides, when you're in a state of terror about your mental health, the last thing you want to feel is confused. 'You're experiencing panic disorder, which is triggered by the threat response in your amygdala. We can try you on a course of benzodiazepines, or maybe propran-olol. Perhaps an ECG too, just to be certain.' *EH?!!*

I wrote about my recovery from a proactive perspective and shared tips that I'd discovered, but up until that point I'd kept it private (except for family). Again, people weren't discussing mental health on social media as openly as they do now. I shared my first public post on Facebook on a Sunday evening, not knowing the impact that it would have. I'd like to say that I agonised over this decision (to make it seem more dramatic), but I didn't; I just clicked 'share'. I was so tired of apologising for something that I couldn't control. Tired of pretending to be fine, because I was afraid of how others might react. I didn't expect abuse – these were, after all, friends and family. Yet, I also didn't expect the sheer volume of direct messages praising my bravery and admitting that they too have experienced mental illness. 'Finally!' An old friend from university messaged. 'I knew you had it too. There were so many times I nearly brought it up. Thank you for being brave enough to write about it. It's inspired me to go and see my doctor.'

'Coming out' was the single most liberating experience of my life.

With the growth of Instagram, Snapchat and LinkedIn, social media quickly became the driving force for spreading mental health awareness and in my opinion still is. Nadiya Hussain famously shared her experiences with panic in an Instagram post in November 2018. She admits that she lives with panic disorder and goes on to say:

I'm sharing this video because as a mother, as a wife, as a 33-year-old woman, I feel like I should have my shit together. Yet there I was helpless again, victim to my anxiety, I could not breathe, move or wash. It was disgusting and embarrassing, and I always feel sad and ashamed that I let it get me again. But today is another day and I am going to try and do as many normal things as is physically possible. For anyone suffering, remember you are not alone, I am with you, so many of us are with you.

An honest and powerful message that many people responded to. Her status as a celebrity made this gesture even braver. After all, 'What does she have to worry about? She's been on *Bake Off*, she must be rich!' Seeing this Instagram post, with her looking raw and exhausted, talking about a 'hidden' condition, was undoubtedly a comfort to thousands – 129,976 to be precise (as is the current views count). Some of the comments include:

Watching this just gave me the motivation to wash properly for the first time in days. Thank you. Today won't be wasted ❤

(This) happened to me too. I was so embarrassed. You are even more of a hero to me now.

You're an amazing person to look up to! Thanks for the words of encouragement.

Honesty is not only empowering to the individual, but to so many suffering in silence. All it takes is for one person to recognise the symptoms and think, 'omg I feel like that too', realise that what they're dealing with is a legitimate condition and BOOM, they're on the path to recovery.

Being open in the real world

Social media is a great platform for spreading awareness, but does it encourage people to be honest in the real world?

Openly discussing panic was something that I wanted to continue offline and I made it my mission to do so. When, for instance, I got my third job in the publishing industry, I saw this as a great opportunity. Rather than hide my condition, I opted to inform my two managers during my probation meeting.

I explained that I'd been diagnosed with social anxiety and panic attacks in 2013, and although it flared up on occasion, it wouldn't affect the quality of my work. I then explained how they might support me if a flare-up did occur, flexible working hours for example, or rearranging meetings. (Always good to tell people what you need, I find.) Both of them were slow to react. Perhaps due to shock.

They asked a lot of questions which I found encouraging. 'I'd never have guessed, Claire. It's obviously easier to hide than I thought.' One of them said, 'It's a real eye-opener. I hate the idea that any member of my team might be struggling in silence.'

It was a positive meeting and I left feeling liberated, but also nauseous because ... I still have fucking social anxiety and this meeting was a big deal! Nothing had really changed, except everything had changed. I'd taken the first step towards total transparency offline and it felt good.

There were times over the following months that I struggled to put my plan into action. After all, I was at management level myself now and felt the pressure to set a good example to the entry level members of staff. But then, what kind of example did I want to set? The 'uber unflappable exec' that had been rolled out for decades, or something new and honest?

I got my chance right before a quarterly sales meeting. I felt a huge panic attack hovering as I walked to the boardroom. *You can't ask them to cancel. It's a monthly meeting. People have travelled from all over the country to attend.* The idea of presenting for more than a few minutes sent me into a spiral of fear. But I'd come this far, and I sure as fuck wasn't going back into the closet. I asked for a quiet word with one of the managers and explained what was happening. 'I'm not asking you to cancel and I've done all of my research to present. I just might need to be honest with the others about how I'm feeling.'

She supported this plan and I told eight people in a boardroom that I was 'having issues with a panic attack that morning, so apologies if it affects my delivery'. *I cannot believe you just did that,* panic spat as I waited in agony for their responses. I was greeted with smiles and a few nods, but the general vibe was 'no worries!' It helped to witness that those people, although sorry for my distress, were there to hear my report, not assess the colour of my cheeks! It takes more balls to be vulnerable than it does to pretend to be OK. In this case reality had outrun fantasy, and experiencing an attack in front of an audience isn't anywhere near as disastrous as I imagined.

Afterwards, I received emails from three of the attendees, one of which read:

> I was really impressed by your honesty today. I've been to mental health seminars before but seeing it in reality and how you dealt with it was much more powerful.
> – **Reema**

I spoke to Omar Latif, the CEO of mental health tech start-up ASSIF about his experiences with stigma and why people sharing their experiences is what will make lasting change. 'The concept of "break the stigma" is all talk and no action, it's too flaky. Change won't happen because they introduce yoga once a month or have a person pop in the office to do a mindfulness class. Change starts with conversations.' This is one of the reasons he has been so open about his own experiences with depression, not only to staff, but to investors also. 'We need to start trusting the people we employ.'

His views are revolutionary, and I couldn't agree more. I've seen greater roads made towards real change by people telling their own stories, or by calling in sick with a mental health problem, rather than blaming it on a stomach bug. According to a recent study conducted by Adzooma, '12.8 million sick days were taken by employees in the UK alone due to a mental health issue. This is estimated to cost businesses between £39.4 billion and £99 billion each year.' Furthermore, '67.9% of people surveyed for the study haven't told their employer about their mental health and 83.3% have no plans to tell them in the future'. Participants for whatever reason didn't feel that the environment was safe to do so.

The irony is that 'coming out' and being honest is what could trigger real and lasting change.

Tom Barker, a PR executive from Essex, made the brave decision to 'come clean' to his boss after a particularly bad flare-up.

We had a person from Mind come in and talk to us about mental health, but she mainly focused on depression, so I was nervous about disclosing my panic disorder to my manager. I'd been working at the agency for nine months and so far it hadn't flared up too badly. However, I had a really bad night with it after a campaign ended and I didn't get a moment's sleep. My nerves were raw, and I didn't trust myself to drive safely. I needed to rest. So, I rang my manager, feeling vulnerable the whole time, and explained what'd happened. While she didn't fully understand the condition, she treated me with respect. The following day, we had a meeting and I explained how panic disorder might affect me sporadically. I also brought her some information to read, that summarised panic disorder better than I did! She made it clear that I was a valued member of her team and that I deserved professional support just like everyone else.

Ultimately, it's a risk to both sides and just as we trust the people we employ, we must also take a chance on those who employ us. Like Tom found out, if you don't take that chance you may never find out and spend years suffering in silence.

Think of it like the parable of the blind people describing an elephant from touch alone. One person touches the trunk and says, 'It's like a snake!' The other touches its leg and says, 'It's like the trunk of a tree!' Another feels its side and says, 'No, it's like a wall!' No matter how many times an elephant is described to a person, they could never truly appreciate what this animal is until they see one. Seeing one makes it real.

Similarly, we won't see any real change in the workplace without people showing their 'crazy'. One person telling the truth can create a Mexican wave movement, and cause a real shift in attitudes.

Even with all of this information, I've stumbled a few times when panic has resurfaced unexpectedly.

During a gig in early 2019, for example, I was completely blindsided. It's not easy to do the brave thing when you're frightened, no matter how much you know it's the right course of action. I'd agreed to do some filming with Salford University who were launching a mental health service for students. I'd done filming many times before, so I didn't expect to be caught off guard. However, as soon as I stepped in that room *I knew*. It's sort of like a sixth sense. I knew that I was going to have an attack as soon as we started filming.

The gig was simple enough. Lucy, the organiser, would ask me some questions on camera, and I would answer them. Yet when the first question was asked, I froze; I could barely remember my name. A new symptom for me, complete brain freeze, and it was unsettling. *This is pathetic, you look so unprofessional. They're paying you to do a job and you're not delivering.* I tried to laugh and said that I had momentary 'stage fright'. Both Lucy and Craig, the cameraman, were very patient, and we started again a few moments later. Once again, panic tightened its grip on my throat, and I couldn't speak. I could hear the words coming out of Lucy's mouth, but my brain couldn't make sense of them. It was as though she was speaking an alien language. 'Sorry, can you reword that?' I snapped, though I didn't mean it to come out as harshly as it did. She looked momentarily confused, but nodded and reframed the question, which I still didn't understand. *What the fuck is going on? Have you now lost the ability to understand English?* My legs felt like jelly and the grey fog began to form across my eyes. *Get out. Get out now. Word will spread that you're a fuck-up and you won't get any more work opportunities.* I could feel tears of humiliation burning my eyes as I walked towards the door. Of all the times I've wanted my medication to stop working and actually allow me to cry, this exact moment, in a professional setting, was not it! If anything, the thought made me feel even more panicked. 'I'm really sorry,' I said. 'I can't do this, I really can't. I won't charge you a penny. I'm so embarrassed. I just don't feel well, and I need to leave.' I all but pounced on my belongings, grappling with the blazer that shrank in the wash. I shoved my arms into the sleeves, and the shirt underneath bunched up uncomfortably, making me feel constricted, like I was in a straitjacket.

Both Craig and Lucy looked concerned, rather than annoyed. 'Is there anything we can do to help?' asked Craig, turning the backdrop light off and approaching me slowly, as though I were a startled horse ready to bolt.

'No, please I just want to go. I'm so sorry.'

'Don't be sorry, you haven't done anything wrong.'

'I've wasted your time. I've never been this unprofessional before.'

'Honestly, you're fine! We had a politician in yesterday who'd clearly had a few pints at lunch and could barely string a sentence together!'

I laughed nervously.

'Is it a panic attack?' Lucy asked.

I nodded and felt the tears forming. 'I'm so embarrassed.'

'If you want to go then you can absolutely do that, nobody is stopping you. But you've done nothing to be embarrassed about. We're filming a mental health video, after all!'

We all laughed at that. The irony of the situation was not lost on us.

While we took a few moments to relax, Craig showed me some photos of his sausage dog, Laurence Longbottom, which was a welcome distraction. In my exposed and vulnerable state, their kindness made me cry even more. I figured that at this point I might as well be honest about how I was feeling. I'd already 'outed' myself.

'My brain is in panic mode,' I said, 'and I can't think straight. I worry that I won't be able to answer the questions unless I literally read the words off a script. I'm sorry for wasting your time.'

Lucy considered this for a moment.

'Well, we have the room booked for another three hours, so there's no rush at all. I'd be happy to make you some cue cards if that would help?'

I stared at her sceptically. 'No, really, you don't have to do that. I should just be able to snap out of this. I'm supposed to be an expert.'

STOP! Why do you find it so hard to accept that you deserve help? Let her help you, just as you helped Ellie all those years ago.

'I'd be happy to.' Lucy continues, 'Being on camera is nerve-racking even for a person who doesn't have a mental health condition.

We want you to be comfortable. It'll only take me ten minutes to make a few cards up. We're a team and we're here to support you, not judge you.'

'If we're all being honest,' added Craig, 'I was really nervous before you arrived today. I haven't been doing this for long and I worried you might notice my inexperience. I couldn't sleep last night I was thinking about it so much!'

'I had three months off with depression last year,' Lucy said. 'I was suicidal at one point. But ever since I came back to work, I feel like I need to "make up" for the time I took by working extra hard. It's bullshit, because I know I wouldn't feel that pressure if it had been a physical illness.'

I was stunned by the change in the atmosphere. How had all three of us gone from stiff, ultra-serious 'professionals' to human within a matter of minutes? Honesty and vulnerability, that's how. It was empowering. Admitting that you're nervous not only takes the sting out of an emotion, but it will trigger empathy in others. Authenticity is a powerful quality that gets overlooked. Brené Brown touches on this in her influential TED talk 'The Power of Vulnerability', where she says: 'We are hard-wired to connect with others, it's what gives purpose and meaning to our lives.' Being vulnerable bonds us and allows us to thrive. It builds trust and understanding. If being vulnerable is a positive thing, then why is it so hard? Because socialisation turned it into a weakness. *Great.* As a society we all 'toughed up', and kept our problems to ourselves. Unfortunately, as psychologist Karen Young points out, 'When we close down our vulnerability, we are shielded from hurt, but we are also shielded from love, intimacy and connection. They come to us through the same door. When we close it to one, we close it to all.'[1]

Personally, it's the risk factor. Allowing my defences to drop opens me up to potential rejection and judgement, something that panic has used to taunt me forever. *Don't say anything, because if you do, they'll think badly of you.* It also relates back to self-love and the relationship I have with myself. 'We love seeing raw truth and openness in other people, but we are afraid to let them see it in us,' Brown writes. 'Vulnerability is courage in you and inadequacy in me.'[2] Yup, that's about right. It's difficult to treat yourself with the same respect you afford to others, yet this is ultimately what'll improve things, both for yourself and for attitudes towards wellbeing in general.

As I stood in front of the camera, with Lucy holding the cards up for me to read, I felt calmer. As always, panic wanted me to keep the attack a secret, to run, to not share how I was feeling. Yet sharing the problem enabled me to not only do a good job but make two new mates in the process.

You can't expect things to change or people to understand if you don't even give them the chance. As a cynic, it can be hard for me to remember this. When you've been let down by people, or institutions that were supposed to help you but failed, it's difficult not to become jaded. Even so, resentment isn't what brings about positive change in the world, it's people, both with kindness and action. They might surprise you given the opportunity. If nothing else, learn to accept help when it's offered. We all need it from time to time, and after that first cringeworthy sixty seconds, it's not so bad.

'Be strong enough to stand alone, smart enough to know when you need help, and brave enough to ask for it.'
Ziad K. Abdelnour

CHAPTER 10

Help! Educating Those Closest to Us

'We need to leave.'

'Eh?'

'We need to leave right now.'

'Why?'

'BECAUSE THERE ISN'T ENOUGH OXYGEN IN HERE! I KNOW IT!'

Scott looks confused. This isn't the first time he's seen me freak out, but even for me, this is extreme.

'Can't you wait until the interval?'

'NO!'

'Well ... It's fine. Claire, I feel fine.'

'That's because you're sucking up my share of the fucking oxygen!'

'How can you be struggling to breathe if you're talking to me?'

I stand abruptly and practically trample over him. I need to get out of here, I need to breach the surface. Trust Scott to pick theatre seats right in the middle of a row. I feel trapped and wobble as I frantically surge forwards. My foot connects with a backpack that's blocking the aisle and I lose my footing. I glare at the owner, who audibly sighs and drags it back under her seat. *Why does everyone look so angry? I can't breathe!* The air feels dry and hot and my entire body is on fire. Sweat pools in my armpits and lower back. Scott says something behind me, but I can't make out the words, I only hear my heartbeat. *This is different, this isn't a panic attack. Am I having a stroke?* I push past two of the ushers and stagger into the corridor, Scott following behind me. 'We ask that people don't leave during the show,' says the younger usher, arms crossed and brow furrowed. 'I can't breathe!' I blurt out. He gives me a look that I've seen many times before. *He thinks I'm on drugs or something.* Not that I give a shit. I barge past him, making my way through the foyer.

Out on the street I breathe deeply; the cool air hits like a soothing tonic and I drink it in. The relief doesn't last long and soon I feel wretched. A mixture of rage and terror.

'Why were they looking at me like that? As though I were some kind of nuisance? How could they not see it?' I cry, stomping away from the theatre.

'Because you look fine,' Scott responds.

I stop and glare at him incredulously. How could he be so ignorant? After all the conversations we've had about mental health.

Realising his mistake and my temper, he clarifies: 'You might be feeling like you're going to explode or whatever, but you look completely normal. Your lips weren't blue, and I didn't see any steam coming out of your ears. You looked fine, I promise. If blood was gushing down your face, or you were foaming at the mouth, then of course I would've done something.'

*

For anyone who's never experienced the sensation of not being able to catch one's breath, I envy you. Imagine being stuck under water, two inches away from the surface, but knowing that you can't reach it. Your lungs burn and your chest muscles contract, and horror grips every inch of your consciousness. It's not something that you forget. Ever.

It's rare that those closest to us will know how to help during a panic attack, often because in the early stages we don't know what is happening to ourselves, let alone how to instruct them. As an irrational disorder, any standard rational responses just make things worse. I've nearly decked several people for telling me to 'calm down'. The equivalent would be to suggest that a person vomiting just 'stop vomiting'. The symptoms of panic can be invisible to others. During some of my worst panic attacks, times when I truly thought I was going to die, nobody around me had a clue that anything was wrong.

'What am I like during a really bad panic attack?' I ask Dan when I get home that evening.

'A complete nightmare,' he responds without missing a beat.

I take a steadying breath and ask him to elaborate.

'You won't keep still or listen, and I feel like everything that I say is wrong.' Thinking he's done, I consider this point, but he continues: 'You're like one of those thrashing, demon cats at the vet that they have to restrain. The really agitated kind. Except, I can't wrap you in a massive towel and restrain you until you calm down. Honestly, it's horrible to watch.'

A demonic cat? That's fair. I'd never really thought about it from Dan's perspective. Although the thought of being swaddled by a giant towel sounds quite pleasant, if it ever comes to that.

By 2017, five people in my life have a 'What to do if Claire is freaking out' guide. At first, I was dubious about creating it. Was I being self-indulgent or foolish? Yet the response was overwhelmingly positive.

'You have no idea how helpless it all makes me feel, watching you go through hell and knowing that I can't help,' Dan said to me. The guide had given him the means to take positive action and help me tackle the attack.

In the early stages of recovery, I had no desire to see things from his perspective. None whatsoever. If anything, I felt contempt towards him and everyone else. Why waste my time when the next attack was probably around the corner? Instead, I preferred to dwell on my internal island of misery, wallowing alone. During the attacks that were so violent they brought me to my knees, I'd lash out verbally when he or anyone else failed to provide comfort. 'Why can't you do something? I don't understand. I can't believe I have to cope with this alone again. Stop telling me to sit down and relax, I fucking can't. I need help!' It seemed unfair.

We expect care and sympathy from those closest to us, that's standard. A Lemsip if we have a cold, or a hot-water bottle and a bar of chocolate if we're on our period. Shared understanding provides relief. It helps us to heal faster and is not only encouraged but expected of medical professionals. In a recent article for in-Training. org (an online peer-reviewed publication for medical students) author Anna Morrow wrote about the importance of having empathy: 'A patient's chart can only reveal so much. When providers have a meaningful conversation with patients, the providers gain a better, more holistic understanding of the patient, determine how to deliver challenging news, decide which information would be especially motivating for treatment, and many other insights that would not be possible without having a great bedside manner.'

How a condition sounds on paper can be very different in reality and will vary depending on the person. My friend Natasha, for example, has experienced panic symptoms that I have not. 'My attacks usually begin with sounds becoming louder and colours brighter than they were just a few seconds before. It's like someone has turned the world up.' My first response to this was confusion: 'Eh? What you on about? That's not a panic attack!' I soon accepted that the symptoms triggered by the amygdala can indeed vary – I do not have the authority on fear.

Despite my desire to be comforted, I consider whether I'd be frustrated if Dan didn't immediately know how to respond to an allergic reaction or if my arm popped out of its socket? Probably not, as he'd never dealt with either scenario, what with them being uncommon. So why did I take it so personally when he couldn't cure my panic? Not just him, my mum couldn't help either (which was especially disconcerting, as she can fix anything). She always knew how to comfort me, but not this time.

In my defence, the rapid and violent onset of panic attacks, and the terror they inspire, causes most people to react emotionally and unable to grasp reason. How can any innocent bystander respond to that, without warning?

I spoke to my friend, journalist Madeleine Spencer, about this. She's been very open about her experiences with panic attacks and living with emetophobia, a fear of vomit. It can be especially difficult for her to fly (I mean in a plane, not alongside Superman).

I was on a flight with my dad and I started to feel panicky. He knows about my condition, but it's not something that we talk about very often. At that moment, a passenger two rows in front of us started to be sick, directly in my eyeline. Knowing that I would freak out, my dad acted quickly. He pushed me forward and declared 'Let me give you a massage!' With my head touching my knees he began vigorously rubbing my neck and back. Although confusing, this was an excellent distraction. I was completely unaware of the vomiting man and my panic attack eased.

While Madeleine's dad's reaction might seem extreme, he clearly reacted on instinct, knowing that Madeleine would become distressed. He sought to control the situation before it could escalate. Like a tourniquet on a puncture wound, it won't solve the problem completely, but it'll slow the process.

Dan, for example, has been known to wave a twenty-pound note in my face if I'm on the verge of a temper tantrum. 'Don't think about X, just look at the money!' (Speaks to the capitalist in me every time!)

Unfortunately, not all interactions with loved ones are positive ones. I spoke to Ryan, a barista and long-time follower of my blog.

I started having panic attacks after a bad experience with drugs at university. My mum doesn't get it at all and won't even try. She's the proper Geordie, strong, no-nonsense type. I had one at Christmas and she didn't react well. We were in the kitchen and I felt it coming. I told her that I couldn't breathe and started to cry. She gave me such a fierce slap across the face and screamed at me to 'get my head straight!' Maybe she thought the 'tough love' approach might help. I'm still angry with her about it, I wish that she would at least try to understand how I feel.

I'm introduced to the work of Dr Lynne Drummond when I write the foreword for the book, *The Female Mind*. In her writing, she details the frustration that friends and family can feel when a loved one experiences panic attacks on a regular basis, particularly when out in public. 'The desire to accuse them of being melodramatic is strong, but such judgement is not only unwarranted, but damaging. We shouldn't presume to understand how another person is feeling.' Snap judgements happen before we've even had time to clock them, but it's better to wait before saying something that you can't take back. (I've learned this lesson the hard way, many times.)

On reflection, I understand people's reaction to panic attacks; they're disruptive after all, not to mention inconvenient. Young children can be excused for crying and rolling around on the floor during an emotional outburst, but adults cannot. Social norms and values dictate that we behave in ways deemed appropriate for society as a whole. Psychologist Dr Marco F. H. Schmidt explains it thus: 'From an early age, they [children] learn from adults the rules that determine everyday social interactions. These norms are like a "social glue" and have played a key role in the evolution and maintenance of human cooperation and culture.'[1] Once we reach a certain age, an individual is expected to compose him/herself and exert control over their emotions. That said, I struggle to keep a rein on my emotions at the best of times, whether I'm having a panic attack or not. For example, when the tube pulls into my station and I can see that it's already rammed. Or when I planned to have avocado on toast for breakfast (and had been looking forward to it all morning) and I go to squeeze the avocado only to find it's rock hard. Not even a hefty splodge of yoghurt can salvage it. I might as well go back to bed. Day RUINED.

'Can't you just have the toast?' Dan asked.

'No, I can't just have the sodding toast! I want the avocado. I was banking on the avocado. I can't believe this is happening to me!' (First ... world ... problems.)

For the record, after the meltdown I did just have the toast, but it was bitter toast. I also toyed with the idea of writing a strongly worded email to Tesco about the emotional impact that hard avocados can inflict on breakfast lovers, but then I had a cup of tea and got over it.

As a direct result of education and social cohesion, adults are conditioned to keep their emotions in check, especially when in public. Unfortunately, panic abides by no such rules. Fear overrides socialisation and reacts with the instinct to protect, regardless of 'causing a scene' or offending.

Said conditioning is probably why those close to us act 'badly' during a panic attack. They too are reacting in response to social norms and, without sharing the fear of the afflicted, can't understand the desire to go against them. Basically, during an attack, I'm the only one freaking out, I'm the only who feels like I'm going to die, and my symptoms aren't visual. The attack comes on quickly, before I have the chance to express myself. So, my anger at what I perceive to be a negative response for observers, is actually ingrained and completely natural. It was MY behaviour that went against the norms that we all abide by, not theirs.

In the short term this is not a comforting thought, and the pressure to 'not draw attention' adds even more pressure. Not to mention guilt and shame.

As Ryan's story indicates, negative reactions from loved ones can be at best frustrating and at worse devastating. Dr Alys Cole King warns readers of statements to be avoided, particularly those that might be perceived of belittling, such as, 'Surely it wasn't that bad!' (Can we just take a moment and imagine saying that to a person who'd just had a stroke?)

In the name of balance, I spoke to Lisa, a mother from Manchester. Her seventeen-year-old daughter has panic attacks in a variety of situations and she struggles to understand.

The first one happened at the supermarket. She started crying and told me that her chest hurt, and she was having a heart attack. Then ran out of the store. There was nothing I could do to comfort her and in the end we had to leave. I was so worried, but at the hospital, the doctor said that there was nothing physically wrong with her. We had blood tests taken and everything. I hoped it was just a fluke. But then she started having these 'episodes' in all sorts of places: restaurants, train stations, anywhere except the house. I asked her about it on several occasions, but she'd get angry when I struggled to understand. I admit, I did wonder whether she was over-exaggerating to get out of attending college.

I finally lost my temper at her grandma's seventieth birthday party. The whole family gathered at a nice restaurant to celebrate and we'd barely sat down before my daughter started begging to leave. I tried everything to soothe her, but she wouldn't stop crying and she wouldn't listen to a word anyone said. Her poor grandma was very upset by the whole thing. In the end I ordered a taxi and just sent her home with the key. I felt guilty afterwards, but a part of me was angry that she hadn't even tried to help herself. I don't know what else to do, we've been to the doctor so many times.

I can sympathise with both points of view. The mother – although irritated – loves her daughter and is distressed on her behalf, but she's seeking to resolve the issue in a way that is counterproductive. The daughter (I imagine) is in pain and feels misunderstood, or even abandoned by her mother. A classic case of miscommunication from both parties.

Some of the things said to me over the years (from various people) include:

- 'Stop it now, you're being silly!'
- 'We all feel stressed now and again, Claire. You really should learn how to deal with it.'
- 'My sister has panic attacks and she isn't this bad.'
- 'Why are you acting so weird?'
- 'I don't know what to say, you're being hysterical.'

None of the above was intended to be hurtful, but they were. They made me feel alienated and exposed. As though I were deliberately courting attention and lacked self-control.

Charities including Time to Change, Anxiety UK and MQ campaign to highlight the common misunderstandings that people have about mental health disorders. Unlike a cold or physical condition, for example, a panic attack isn't always visibly obvious. Professor John Powell has written about the difficulties of spotting panic attack distress signals and how it's important for the afflicted to tutor close ones, so that they can be of assistance the next time panic strikes.

For me, it wasn't enough to have compassion from others. Empathy without understanding is about as useful as a boat without a paddle. I needed to help those around me to give me what I needed.

More than anything I wanted to be understood. I wanted those closest to me to know how panic made me feel, not just the attack itself, but the lead-up to it, and the aftermath. I wanted permission to let go and fall apart. I'd spent so much time feeling like I needed to shield them from the thoughts and various mood swings. I'd laugh it off and claim that I was just 'being daft', meanwhile battling with panic in isolation. I was tired of feeling like a burden, and continually apologising for something that I had little control over was demoralising. Or as professor and author Leon F. Seltzer, PhD writes: 'Without experiencing that others know us, or are *able* to, we're left feeling alone – at times, despairingly so. It's a bleak place to be and can lead to feelings of emptiness and despondency.[2]

So, what the fuck did I want then? What would help during an attack? Clearly wallowing and shouting abuse wasn't doing the trick. During quiet periods, I devoted time to pondering this. From previous experiences that ended up (by fluke) being positive, I knew that I liked it when people took charge of the situation. This made me feel secure. The worst thing to do is ask me lots of questions, such as 'Why do you think this is happening?' Or argue with the sweeping statements that come out of my mouth. 'What do you mean you feel like the ceiling is about to collapse, Claire? It isn't.' *OF COURSE I FUCKING KNOW THAT DEEP DOWN, KATHRYN! But I'm freaking out right now, please don't ask me to explain the intricacies behind my ramblings, when I can hardly see straight!*

It's better if the person acknowledges that I'm having a panic attack, reminds me that I'm safe and not embarrassing myself, then either makes me laugh, or distracts me. Don't fuss, don't draw more attention to me and don't freak out yourself, just let the time pass.

My brother (through no effort on his part, I might add) is excellent when an attack strikes. *You're having a panic attack? That's shit.* He then either changes the subject, or suggests we stick the kettle on. Boom, job done. Acceptance, sympathy and decisive action without making me feel like I'm being a bother or creating a scene. This helps to reframe the scene in my mind; despite the internal noise, panic isn't as noteworthy as I believe it to be. During one brutal attack, early in my recovery, we did step-aerobics at midnight on the Nintendo Wii. He didn't point out the lateness of the hour, or that being in our late twenties we were probably too old for this shit. We just ate Mini Cheddars and stepped.

In fairness, my brother has an unfair advantage as he's known me his entire life and spent twenty years observing my emotional out-bursts and erratic behaviour. In contrast to me, he's a very calm person. I like to think that I panic for both of us.

For those without the advantage of being my immediate sibling, I needed to communicate my needs clearly, concisely and in advance.

The idea to create a written guide struck me when I was at the pharmacist. I noticed a leaflet highlighting the symptoms of a stroke and how a bystander should act. Perhaps I could do something simi-lar for my panic attacks?

What would that acronym look like? I wonder.

PLEASE stay fucking calm

ACCEPT that I'm freaking out and offer brief sympathy

NOW remind me that I can breathe, I'm not having a heart attack, I won't shit myself and that everything is going to be fine

IGNORE your instincts to tell me to 'calm down'

COMEDY – think fast and make me laugh!

Knowledge is a powerful thing and being proactive allowed me to once again take back control. So that's what I did. Inspired by the leaflet, I went home and created my own. I still have the original copy somewhere.

What is a panic attack?

A panic attack is the abrupt onset of intense fear or discomfort. It is not something that I can control or stop once it's been triggered. In order to relate to this fear, imagine a time in which you've nearly (or have) fallen downstairs, and the sudden rush of panic and loss of control you feel.

What symptoms do I experience?

Physical

- Pounding heart
- Feeling as though I can't breathe
- Feeling detached from my body
- Dizziness
- Nausea
- Numb/heavy limbs
- Sweating
- Dry mouth
- Tremors in my hands
- Difficulty seeing and hearing

Mental and emotional

- I feel as though liquid terror has been injected into my veins
- I feel like I'm either going to die or go crazy
- I have the urge to run away
- I cannot calm down, no matter how hard I try

How can you help when I'm having one?

- Remain neutral and grounded. Don't fuss, overreact or tell me to 'relax'
- Distract me with conversation, but DON'T ask too many questions
- Do some breathing techniques with me
- Suggest that we go for a walk
- Make me laugh
- Remind me that I got through previous attacks, so I will get through the one I'm having right now

'Let's go for a walk,' Dan says in a matter-of-fact way, as though it's not nearly midnight and I haven't been pacing around the living room hyperventilating.

'It's eleven forty!' I snap, panic making my tone harsh.

'So? Rigby could do with a quick stroll she's been asleep most of the day, the lazy cow. Besides, walking always helps.'

I'm surprised by his observation. Turns out that I hadn't been the only one compiling panic attack relief tricks.

'Venting helps you too. When you stabilise a bit, tell me what you're afraid of. It'll take the edge off.'

This idea doesn't thrill me. *If you talk about the symptoms, then they'll be real, and you'll lose control.* Still, I do as he asks. The air outside is cold as it hits my lungs and I savour the sensation. I walk, and panic walks with me, but so do Rigby and Dan. Rigby isn't impressed by her late-night stroll, but she begrudgingly complies. 'I'm afraid that I can't cope with this,' I state, 'I'm afraid that my lungs will explode, or I'll pass out and die.'

He doesn't argue with my statements directly but points out, 'You know what this is and you know how to handle it. No matter what *IT* tells you, this is no different from any of the other attacks and it'll pass, it always does. ALWAYS.'

We walk down our street, past the house with all the Betty Boop memorabilia. Stickers on the window, lights and there's even a life-size statue of the lady herself in the driveway. I've never seen the occupants, only Betty. On the main road the local kebab shop is lit up and I see people placing their orders. There's something about the world continuing as normal in spite of me and my panic that I find soothing. It reminds me that there are limits to fear's power.

'What number are we at?' Dan asks, referring to our 1–10 panic scale.

'An eight.'

We continue walking.

'Don't you ever get tired of all this?' I ask.

'No more than you get tired of dealing with all of my neuroses.' (He has his fair share.)

'They barely last more than fifteen minutes these days. You're a pro at dealing with them.'

I consider this and realise that he's right. I spend so much time criticising myself for having attacks, I forget how far I've come.

Back home, he removes his trainers and gets me an ice lolly from the freezer. 'It'll help with the dry mouth.' My mouth is like sandpaper and I'm grateful for the gesture.

I move to give him a hug, mindful not to step on his bare feet in my Chelsea boots. We watch TV for a while and snuggle on the couch in silence. It's nice, and I relish the normality.

I can handle the attacks by myself, I have done hundreds of times, but it's nice to have a little company.

CHAPTER 11

Gut Instinct: Looking After Your Brain with Food

The stomach and the brain are connected. I have this realisation with my head hanging over a fancy toilet bowl.

In thirty minutes' time, I'm due to appear on *BBC Breakfast* with Naga Munchetty and Charlie Stayt. I've no idea why I agreed to this … except I do: I want to be able to say that I've been on the BBC and I've already told far too many people about it. *You're a fucking idiot and this is the price that you pay for vanity. Never mind 'I only ever do media gigs because I want to spread awareness about mental health' because on this occasion you just wanted to be on the telly!*

The BBC is a topsy-turvy place as it turns out. One centred around chaos, overworked runners and rules (so many rules). They also have a habit of making it sound like they're doing YOU a favour, while dragging you out of bed at 4 a.m. and making it clear that if you refer to anything commercial (book, blog, charity associations) they will be very cross.

Back in the toilets, I wash my hands thoroughly, before heading to have my make-up done. Stress vomiting is nothing new to me, I have a habit of throwing up before nerve-racking situations and have done so ever since I was a teenager. It's the reason why I don't have large meals before events or parties, because I know the contents of my stomach won't hold.

The *BBC Breakfast* interview goes well, and I leave the studio with my face a different colour to my neck. I'll never get used to TV make-up, though I deeply respect the process. Make-up artists also have the best chat. Better than a shrink in some ways.

Mum (who I dragged along for support) got told off for taking pictures of me mid-interview, but as she told me afterwards, 'My daughter's on the telly, what did they expect? Besides I'm sixty and retired now, so I don't give a shit!'

I'm heading for the lifts, when one of the assistants offers me a coffee and asks if I can chat for a moment. Coffee is the last thing I want, but after Mum's rebellion in the studio, I don't want to appear rude. So, I accept with a smile. As a rule, I'm aware that the consumption of coffee isn't advised if you have anxiety, and I know about its effects on cortisol levels. Yet, I never truly gave it too much thought. Giving up caffeine hadn't cured my anxiety/panic in the long run, so what harm could it really do? On a full stomach, the answer to this is not much. Unfortunately, thanks to my earlier experience in the toilets, my stomach is emptier than a high street during the coronavirus pandemic. I'm wiped out; the adrenaline that buzzed through my veins earlier is now completely spent. Matthew the assistant ushers me towards a brightly coloured sitting area and promptly returns with the drinks. I take a sip of the hot, dark liquid and then another. It tastes bitter and charred.

'Have you done much radio?' he asks, interrupting my thoughts. 'I'm working on a show for Radio Manchester and I think you'd be a great guest.'

I begin to answer, but I'm distracted by the churning in my stomach. It bubbles and cramps and a rush of heat sweeps over me like a wave. No longer tired, I'm alert: dangerously and uncomfortably alert. My eyeballs feel dry and my heart is pounding. *Am I having another panic attack?*

Not wanting to embarrass myself, or indeed poor Matthew, I squeeze my fists into tight balls and answer. 'Yes, I've done a few shows in London. I'd be delighted to be a guest. Perhaps you could email me about it?'

I'm desperate to end the conversation, but Matthew is passionate about mental health and continues to chat animatedly. My brain sparks and backfires, practically humming with activity. Are my arms twitching? They jerk awkwardly as I reach for my bag. *Is this the coffee? How has it gone straight to my head so fast?* I'm struggling to hang on to a rational thought for more than a second.

For every panic attack I've had, before the heart palpitations, shallow breathing, or anything else that follows, the first warning tends to come from my stomach. The severity varies, from a tingling or 'butterflies' to full-blown nausea. It cramps, wrenches and bubbles, refusing to be ignored. The palpitations, shallow breathing and other symptoms follow close behind, but the stomach is the hub.

Safe at home, I think about my double epiphany at the BBC. The initial flirtation with the stomach–brain connection theory has now morphed into obsession. Nausea and feeling the need to void one's bowels during panic is a survival tactic deployed by the amygdala. The body purges itself of extra weight to aid with flight. In this instance, the brain sends a message to the stomach and the stomach responds. However, I wonder, was this a two-way messenger service?

Was the stomach alerting the brain of trouble? Prompting the amygdala into action?

Doctors have continually suggested that a change in diet might have a positive impact on my mental health. Or at least they did in the months following my nervous breakdown. At the time, I was unwilling to listen to the point of being obnoxious. When one believes that one almost died, one is hardly likely to listen to the bloke banging on about eating more fruit! I appreciate that an apple a day is supposed to do wonders, but I doubt it can stave off the Grim Reaper. Never have I heard of a patient experiencing a heart attack being offered a juicy Granny Smith and a nice cup of tea. It hardly seems appropriate. The same applies for broken bones, migraines, kidney infections, cancer, the list is endless. In the immediate aftermath of an injury or a diagnosis, patients with physical ailments receive medical treatment, as opposed to lifestyle advice; contrast that with patients with mental ailments – they receive lifestyle advice first, medical treatment later.

I wanted the drugs and therapy, not my five a day. In my opinion, there was something intensely wrong with my brain and only hardcore treatment could fix it. I was desperate and I wanted something radical. Dr Soph tells me that this is common. 'Patients who experience panic are more likely to progress quickly in treatment because they'll do anything not to feel the way that they're feeling.' This was certainly true of me. During this period, I can list multiple things that I would've been willing to try if they guaranteed results against panic. Things that would horrify me now. Such as:

- Cage-diving with great white sharks. In fact, I might even do it without the cage

- Bungee-jumping naked, attached to Donald Trump
- Rudimentary ECT – like the proper barbaric *One Flew Over the Cuckoo's Nest* treatment
- Open-mic comedy in front of a hostile crowd with zero prep
- Eating common garden slugs like lollipops for dinner
- Removing each of my nails, straight from the cuticles, with a rusty pair of pliers

Based on such extremes, it's hardly surprising that 'diet' failed to give me a hard-on for self-care.

After the BBC incident, I was forced to consider some hard truths about my food consumption habits, both before and after panic attacks.

We left the studio at eleven o'clock, and by eleven thirty I was downing a glass of white in an attempt to balance out the massacre in my veins, triggered earlier by the black coffee. The waiter poured two glasses, but after he left, I necked mine in one and reached desperately for Mum's. 'I need something to level me out!' I gasped, feeling disgusted with myself.

She nodded and quietly perused the menu, saying nothing. Far from being an enabler, my mum is an anchor, a very wise one. She's the type of person who observes, coming to her own conclusion before starting to lecture me. She understands my actions but knows when to cut me off. 'We'll order some pasta,' she stated. 'You'll need something substantial in your stomach after such a stressful start.' This isn't a suggestion, or request. She'd been up since four thirty herself and yet showed no sign of strain.

So, I drank my wine and ate my pasta like a good girl, while silently thanking her for being by my side (and for paying for lunch!).

I talked manically throughout, word vomit spewing from my mouth as I processed how I was feeling. She ordered water and I drank a large glass, enough to satisfy her, then we decided to walk home. It was twenty minutes away and I needed the exercise. I'm like a dog in that sense. Once home, I sleep for several hours, or rather, I pass out from exhaustion on the couch.

The lecture comes later in the evening, as we watch *The Crown*. 'You can't keep living in such extremes, Claire. It's not healthy. You'll come a cropper one day.' She's not just referring to today; my whole lifestyle was chaotic during that period.

I think it's accurate to say that I've always felt 'wired' after eating. I noticed this more when I joined the working world with its scheduled lunch breaks. My colleagues would report feeling sluggish in the afternoon, whereas I was hyper. Bizarre, but I never questioned it. It was a nuisance to my work because I couldn't focus or contribute anything valid for up to an hour after consuming food. My brain was preoccupied, and I felt on edge. I also noticed that food was related to the panic attacks I had at night. I looked at my eating habits before bed in correlation to night panic. There was a clear pattern that I'd been ignoring for years: if I ate anything heavy less than two hours before I slept, then I'd have an attack.

Here's a classic example of a stomach-related panic attack that caught me off guard in early 2020. I was up at 5 a.m. to write, galvanised by my ideas and blissfully happy with the silence. There's something about those peaceful hours between 5 and 7 a.m. before everyone wakes up that I find magical. I had a coffee to 'get me going', nothing too strong, just a little buzz to remove the fog. It did the trick and I wrote solidly for sixty minutes. So, I had another, why not? Then a third when Dan got up for work. The third was a mistake, which I tried to rectify with two cheese-twist pastries from Tesco. Job done. Then I worked all through the afternoon and by 5 p.m., I realised that I was starving and it was affecting my mood. I ate half a pizza at great speed. Again, job done. But I felt bloated and uncomfortable after consuming it and an hour later, I felt as though a brick had been lodged somewhere between my stomach and my chest. The weight was distracting, and my belly expanded as if I was in the early stages of pregnancy. *Something's wrong.* The weight on my chest was growing, constricting my breathing with each cycle, like a boa constrictor, cutting my breath short and making it difficult to inhale. With my vast knowledge of panic, I tried to comfort myself. *You know what this is. It's a panic attack. I'm not sure what has triggered it, but you will get through it.* The stunted and aggressive breathing was new to me. I was used to immediate hyperventilation, breathing rapidly without result. This felt more sinister, as though I were being slowly crushed to death. My face felt stiff and my limbs turned to jelly, like my motor skills had been compromised. *Is this a stroke? Are my lungs caving in?* I couldn't bear to sit still for any longer and jumped out of my chair. Dan appeared from the shower, talking about the new chest of drawers he'd assembled, and though I tried to be distracted for a moment, I just couldn't stand the symptoms any longer. 'I'm going for a walk!' I snapped. 'Having a bad one, just need to walk it off.' Teetering close to the edge of hysteria, I grabbed my coat, wrapped up warm and headed out the door. I knew it was hysteria because I suddenly felt the urge to spew my guts up, and the idea of doing it in public didn't concern me! Only as I stepped through the door did it occur to me that today's food intake was the problem. It was a light bulb moment and I felt frustrated that something so obvious had passed me by.

'Are you working too hard again?' asked Dan cautiously when I returned.

'No! I drank three coffees back to back and then flittered between starving myself and consuming nothing but heavy white carbs. Of course, my gut is protesting. It must be a chemical storm down there!'

There was the proof, experienced first-hand. It would appear that the stomach does have a direct hotline to the brain. *Fancy that.*

According to Harvard Health: 'A troubled intestine can send signals to the brain, just as a troubled brain can send signals to the gut.' Anthony L. Komaroff goes on to say, 'The very thought of eating can release the stomach's juices before food gets there.' In basic terms, the stomach is like a second brain, sensitive to emotion. There are 100 million neurons in the gut, interacting with gut bacteria and carrying messages to and from the brain. So, if something is out of whack in the gut, then it's going to have an impact on the brain, potentially triggering anxiety or panic. 'Given how closely the gut and brain interact, it becomes easier to understand why you might feel nauseated before giving a presentation or experience intestinal pain during times of stress.'[1]

I consider myself to be a reasonably healthy eater, most of the time. I consume my five a day, avoid copious amounts of sugary foods and drink plenty of water. Previous research on nutrition taught me that certain foods aid the production of serotonin (an enzyme which I and many people with anxiety/panic lack), and that junk food has little to zero nutritional value. But part of me has always questioned why such things about nutrition are certainties?

Don't expect me to blindly believe commercial slogans such as: 'you are what you eat' or 'your body is a temple' without some kind of explanation.

Of course, then along came the whole misleading packaging scandal, the campaign against processed food and the horrors of the meat industry. I'm pro education when it comes to health, but fuck, I wasn't sure what I could eat any more besides raw vegetables. Sorry, raw, organic, locally sourced vegetables. When did things get so complicated?

Not to mention competitive. I'm wary of the 'healthy lifestyle' movement, due to the commercial aspect, the social media shaming and the so-called 'food porn' (which I have myself fallen prey to). Superfood salads look beautiful, they really do, with all those colours and a light sprinkling of pomegranate seeds, but sometimes I just want cheese on toast with a cherry Coke, WITHOUT a side order of shame. Being mindful about what we put into our bodies is good, but I don't want to be consumed by it. Isn't there enough to feel guilty about? Orthorexia (a disorder that involves an unhealthy obsession with healthy eating) is real. In a 2018 article for *Vogue*, journalist Jancee Dunn queried whether orthorexia was 'the eating disorder for the digital age.' 'A 2017 study published in the journal *Eating and Weight Disorders* found a link between Instagram use and orthorexia.' Basically, we all got hooked on the hashtag #cleaneating and popular feeds from wellness entrepreneurs like Ella Mills. This resulted in widespread food guilt. (For the record, Ella really didn't deserve the backlash she received. The poor woman was just using her Instagram to highlight how much she love chickpeas, not to demand that we all love them too!)

Coined by Colorado physician Steven Bratman, MD in 1997, othorexia is still, however, difficult to quantify officially. Many organisations (as of 2020), such as the American Psychiatric Association, do not recognise it as an eating disorder or mental health condition. Therefore, it has not been studied as much as other eating disorders.

The narrative that surrounds healthy eating seems elitist to me, excluding and judging those unable to go to extremes, or invest in luxury products. *Why don't you try consuming nothing but green juice for a week?* Well, because I don't want to be fucking miserable, Jessica! *You should try this retreat in Sweden. It's the best way to detox.* No problem, let me magic together a grand for the flights. The concept of clean eating is very different to the reality, and has become needlessly overcomplicated. I mean, technically a home-made Victoria sandwich cake could be considered 'clean' if it was made using the finest organic flour and free-range eggs, couldn't it?

As a rule, I eat a balanced diet and try to avoid processed foods. A first step towards this would be by taking an interest in ingredients and really think about what we're putting in our bodies. Salt, for example. We add it without question, and it's generally loaded into processed foods. Yet, consider the repercussions. High blood pressure is a direct result of too much salt consumption and is projected to affect more than 1.5 billion people around the world by 2025. How many older people do you know with high blood pressure? I can count at least seven in my inner circle. According to the British Heart Foundation, 'a staggering 75 per cent of the salt that we eat is added before it even goes into our shopping baskets.' The issue isn't that we're ingesting salt, but that we don't know how much we're ingesting.

I'm not suggesting that you stop including it in meals, as who doesn't love a bit on chips? But be mindful about the alternatives. For example, cumin is a great substitute, as is turmeric. Don't cut it out and be miserable, just behave yourself!

Food and serotonin

Serotonin is a compound that we're all born with. If you don't have enough then the only way to resolve this is with medication. This is what I believed for half a decade. It's one of the reasons why I started taking the medication sertraline in the first place.

My dear friend Chloe Brotheridge, anxiety expert and self-confessed gut obsessive, set me straight. It's true that antidepressant medication sertraline (which I'd been taking for years to help with anxiety and panic) is designed to help increase levels of serotonin in the brain. However, the gut can actually produce this naturally, if the conditions are right. Consequently, having healthy bacteria in the gut is important to keep serotonin levels stable. I look into this myself and the evidence is overwhelming. A 2019 study of the gut's microbiota, conducted at the university of California, estimated that a whopping 90 per cent of the body's serotonin is produced in the gut, making gut health and maintaining the levels of 'good' bacteria imperative: 'Previous studies from our lab and others showed that specific bacteria promote serotonin levels in the gut.'[2]

Working with the probiotics company Symprove, whose water-based supplement helps support the gut microbiome, gave me even more insight into the science. 'A 2017 study found that mice raised without gut bacteria were found to display an increase in anxiety-like behaviour. This study found that gut bacteria had an impact on molecules called miRNAs in the amygdala – the part of the brain responsible for the fight-or-flight response which is often very active when we're anxious. MiRNAs are molecules which control how genes are expressed, and the researchers believe this is one way that our gut bacteria can affect our mental health.'[3]

Then Chloe delivers the sucker punch. 'Alcohol depletes serotonin.' I sort of always knew this but had chosen to turn a blind eye up until this point, I loved the dopamine hit too much. It helped 'take the edge off'.

While 2018 saw the rise of the 'sober' movement on social media, which has continued to grow, ironically it made me want to drink even more. I don't like to be bullied or shamed into anything, I said it about *Breaking Bad* and I'll say it again about giving up booze: NO.

Side note – the definition of alcoholism (previously alcoholic) is as follows: 'Alcoholism is when one can no longer control their use of alcohol, compulsively abuse alcohol, despite its negative ramifications, and/or experience emotional distress when they are not drinking.'[4] Sobriety for those with alcoholism is the ultimate goal, not to mention a constant battle. So, it seems bizarre, disrespectful even, that a trend has emerged on social media (mainly from the commercial aspect of the sobriety movement) for those not living with alcohol addiction to post about how many days 'sober' they are. Addiction is an illness to be respected, not a fad. If you decide to give up alcohol, then 'drink free' or 'alcohol free' are more respectful ways of highlighting such a great achievement.

Still, even with all my strong opinions, I couldn't deny that I'd fallen into some bad habits with regards to the 'demon drink'. Over the years, a trip down the pub with friends after a long day generally worked wonders. Not to mention the power that a crisp glass of Chardonnay had to soften gnawing anxiety.

Sure, I could go for a run to ease the strain, or listen to a thirty-minute meditation app, but I'm lazy. I'm also impatient, which made the dart to the pub or my fridge seem like the better option.

Unfortunately, I also couldn't deny the hell that is my brain in the morning if I have more than two glasses. Random fact, a hangover is one of the most common triggers of panic attacks in people who have never previously experienced anxiety. My friend Jane had her first attack at the age of thirty-two. She'd attended a colleague's leaving drinks the night before and got completely smashed. On top of this, she didn't get enough sleep. I woke to several messages: 'I can't breathe. I can't get on the tram. Is this a panic attack?' Yes, Jane, I'm afraid it is.

After a few wines I'd wake up foggy but also uneasy, like I'd done something wrong but wasn't sure what. Inappropriate phone message? No. Naked Instagram post, or worse, a cringeworthy DM to someone you've never met but feel like you'd be great mates if you did? No, thank fuck. An expensive online purchase? No again. So, what is it and why do I feel so edgy? Well, because as Chloe gently explains, we need serotonin to keep the brain functioning anxiety- and panic-free. Sort of like fuel for a car. Like putting diesel in unleaded only, guzzling a chemical that kills something I already don't have enough of seems ludicrous. I'll admit this: I wanted to make a positive change, without feeling as though I was punishing myself.

I also spoke to the dietician (and legend) Laura Tilt about food and nutrition and got to grips with the basics. For instance, I'd always known that oily fish was good for the brain, but I didn't actually really understand why. She explained it to me perfectly: 'If you took your brain and squeezed out all the water, 60 per cent of what is left would be fat – and a good percentage of this is omega-3, a type of fat that helps your brain cells send messages effectively. A number of studies have linked low intakes of omega-3 with an increased risk of depression and anxiety. Humans can't make omega-3, so we have to get it from our diet. Aim to eat oily fish two to three times a week. Other healthy fats found in nuts, seeds, avocados, and olive oil also seem protective.'

Laura also maintains that anything rich in fibre will help 'good bacteria' grow in the gut. So, basically go for wholegrain instead of white; oats are good too and so are seeds – I sprinkle chia seeds on my porridge in the morning. They're inexpensive, don't taste of anything and are packed with both fibre and omega-3. Fruit and veg don't have to be expensive or time-consuming to prepare either. I use frozen blueberries, and half the veg I buy goes in the freezer.

Have you ever wondered why coffee works so well as a laxative? Well, because it produces cortisol (the stress hormone) and we already know that stress encourages the bowels to purge themselves in order to make the body lighter. Put simply, caffeine is liquid panic.

I used to think that coffee made me more productive, but it actually just gave me a buzz. I was wired, but couldn't harness that extra energy in an effective way. Laura informs me that coffee absolutely batters the gut (hence its laxative effect) and disrupts the production of chemicals beneficial to the brain.

All right, so as an all-or-nothing person, I decided that the best way to test the impact of diet on the brain was a complete overhaul. I'd cut out booze for a month, along with caffeine, bread and pasta. *Sorted, job done.* The first day was fine, uneventful – I didn't miss anything and felt rather smug come bedtime. The second day, however, was somewhat different ... in that by late afternoon I was ready to consume a pint of wine with ground coffee mixed into it and a line of sugar on the side. I felt miserable, not to mention short-tempered and lethargic. Also, how long are the evenings without a vice?

Healthline's Jillian Kubala, MS, RD writes that: 'If the body becomes dependent on caffeine, eliminating it from the diet can cause withdrawal symptoms that typically begin 12–24 hours after stopping caffeine. Caffeine withdrawal is a recognised medical diagnosis and can affect anyone who regularly consumes caffeine.'[5]

I was in withdrawal and the symptoms were rough. Still, not one to be defeated I gritted my teeth and stuck it out. Everything surrounding panic so far had taught me that things tend to get worse before they get better. I found that the key is to have a good distraction. (Meaning I went to the gym a lot after work, to spare Dan my rages!)

It wasn't an overnight fix, but by the middle of week three I noticed a few improvements: the reduction in carbs improved my digestion and I didn't feel as bloated or wired after meals. I was sleeping better, and the infamous morning 'brain fog' cleared. I also didn't wake up feeling anxious, or wretched.

But ... I was bored. Is it wrong to admit that publicly? I've read so many testimonials from people who gave up alcohol/caffeine/sugar and found a new lust for life, and I'm desperately jealous. I never experienced that. At one point I gave up alcohol for three months out of curiosity; with the exception of hangovers, I noticed little to no improvements at all. I was still the same me, with the same interests, just without booze.

Therefore, if extreme diets/lifestyle changes weren't the answer then maybe moderation was a safer bet? Annoyingly obvious, but moderation tends to get bypassed by everyone, because it's as old as time! There's nothing new or sexy about it.

By adopting this approach and recognising that alcohol was my biggest vice, I needed to face some home truths about why I drank so much. Yes, it was partly out of habit, but I realised that I also drank to quickly repress uncomfortable emotions, which would eventually dissipate on their own. *You feel anxious? A gin and tonic will get rid of that.* I made a real effort to note down my thoughts and emotions whenever I felt tempted. *This is too much pressure, you need something to take the edge off.* It was almost a reflex that I'd never thought to challenge before.

Moving forward, when the urge for a sip of wine crept in, I would ask myself: 'Do I really want the wine, or can I tolerate this feeling for ten minutes?' The answer was always yes. It was uncomfortable, but I could sit with it and, like a panic attack, I floated through the emotion. Finding a replacement helped too. I got semi-obsessed with trashy historical romance around this time, some of which bordered on erotica. It distracted me as well as wine did and I didn't have to deal with the repercussions. I also had great fun with the book titles. (I swear, in another life, I'm coming back as the person who thinks up titles for erotic fiction!)

As a further boost I implemented the advice that Shahroo Izadi, author of *The Kindness Method*, imparts in her book. Rather than berating myself when the urge to drink struck, I would ask myself a serious of pre-planned questions:

Will one more really make this night more fun?
Do I want to have a panic attack tomorrow?
Do I want to feel like I'm about to have a panic attack tomorrow?
Do I want to feel like a shit human being without knowing why?

This worked a treat. The idea being that I'm not punishing myself – I can have a drink if I want one, it's my decision. However, this approach encourages mindful drinking and taking a moment to think before deciding, rather than blindly bingeing. It's been a positive change for both my brain and my gut, not to mention my bank balance.

Do I still drink? Yup. Have I got drunk since making this change? Or eaten too much bread? Or put sugar in my tea when I needed it? Yup, I'm still human and I like to indulge on occasion, or after a long week. The difference is I have a better rein on my self-control now and how often I allow this to happen. I respect my brain too much these days to knowingly treat it badly.

CHAPTER 12

Night Panic

*I*f you fall asleep, you'll die.

I had this thought for the first time in bed at my parents' house. I was dozing, just drifting off, when suddenly my entire body twitched violently. I sat up, heart pounding furiously and scanned the room, looking for a threat. Dan hadn't come to bed yet, so I didn't have to explain the bizarre outburst to him. I lay back down and tried to steady my breathing. It was probably just 'one of those things', a trick of the fantasy realm similar to 'tripping' or 'falling' in the early stages of a dream and waking up with a jolt. This is referred to as a 'hypnic jerk' or 'sleep start'. The movement is involuntary, like hiccups, or a random pulsating twitch below the eye. Upon researching this further, I found that there aren't any concrete explanations for this night-time abnormality (typical of most mental health research), but I did come across some interesting theories. Psychologist Tom Stafford explains:

> They [hypnic jerks], represent the side effects of a hidden battle for control in the brain that happens each night on the cusp between wakefulness and dreams.

Normally we are paralysed while we sleep. Even during the most vivid dreams our muscles stay relaxed and still, showing little sign of our internal excitement.

Instead, hypnic jerks seem to be a sign that the motor system can still exert some control over the body as sleep paralysis begins to take over. Rather than having a single 'sleep–wake' switch in the brain for controlling our sleep (i.e. ON at night, OFF during the day), we have two opposing systems balanced against each other that go through a daily dance, where each has to wrestle control from the other.[1]

In a nutshell, the rational part of the brain sometimes struggles to let go of the reins and exerts its power by waking you up with a jolt.

Another theory dates back to our primate ancestors. Psychologist Frederick Coolidge, has suggested that a hypnic jerk could be: 'an archaic reflex to the brain's misinterpreting the muscle relaxation accompanying the onset of sleep as a signal that the sleeping primate is falling out of a tree'.[2]

This would explain why on the rare occasions that I have fallen asleep on public transport, I wake almost immediately with a jump, freaking out the person sitting next to me. The brain recognises that this is not a safe place to lose consciousness and acts.

'Like "the kick" scene in the film *Inception*?' Dan asked when I shared the theory with him. The best way to explain anything to my husband is with a film reference. 'Exactly like that!' The brain needs to wake up a person quickly and therefore pushes said person off a kerb or makes them fall off a building.

Dan and I had moved into my parents' house several months earlier, to save a deposit for a house of our own. If we wanted to achieve this goal before the age of sixty, then leaving London was a necessity. They'd relocated to Germany, so it made sense to live in a free house with no rent, bills, or any real responsibility besides cleaning it once a week (fortnightly, let's be honest). A dream opportunity, on paper, at least.

I had forgotten how many ghosts reside in that house. I didn't consider the history, memories and overall vibe of the place when I decided to move in.

I left for a reason in 2012. I wasn't happy. Not because I was a 'tortured soul' with a pocket full of dreams and a desire to work in Hollywood. But I was very aware of the limitations of my surroundings. The lack of creative opportunities, for example, and culture. Previous generations were told to get a job at a good company and work your way up over the course of a decade. Being fulfilled at work was considered a luxury, rather than a genuine goal. I knew this way of living wasn't going to work for me, but I kept those thoughts to myself.

In order to be happy, I need to be stimulated both intellectually and creatively. I like variety, diversity and to be around people/places I find inspiring. I used to be ashamed of this, fearing that my desire for adventure and fulfilment made me seem egocentric. I worried that others would take offence, thinking that my wanting something different made me critical of their choices. It's an impossible thought cycle, which I eventually let go of when I lived in London. Ambition, I learned, can be a good thing. I knew what I wanted, and I went for it.

Despite being successfully self-employed as a writer for three years, back home people still asked how much longer I reckoned it would last. And what my plans would be when it 'all dried up'.

There was something about being back in my hometown that made me uncomfortable.

My 2012 move to London to work in publishing was a great personal achievement, and despite what happened, I still wouldn't change anything.

But the Claire who'd last lived in this house was incredibly unhappy. Her social anxiety demons were born and developed here, not to mention her self-torture tendencies.

I agreed to the move because it was the right decision for our future. We'd been married for a year and it was time to 'grow up', so to speak. But I don't think either of us thought it through enough (his entire family is based in London). I'd also left a lot behind: my London friends, mental health network, work connections and opportunities. London was 'only two hours away, after all'. I could travel there and back for work easily in a day.

Besides, how dare I feel anything but grateful? We'd been offered a rent-free house with a huge garden for fuck's sake! I was frustrated with myself for being so negative.

So, on 22 May 2017, the day of the tragic Manchester bombings to be exact, we moved, and within two months the night panic attacks started.

12 July 2009

My brother nearly died on his twenty-first birthday. He went 'gorge-jumping' with friends and something went terribly wrong. Gorge-jumping involves climbing waterfalls and then hurling yourself into deep pools, which is apparently a pleasurable activity.

Would it be trite to say that I knew something awful was going to happen that day? I watched him leave and something just felt 'off'. Perhaps I'm an oracle of some sort, with hidden abilities? Or maybe my amygdala, knowing what a dangerous fucking activity gorge-jumping is, felt threatened by proxy.

So, when the phone rang at 5 p.m. that Saturday afternoon, I knew exactly who it was, and I knew what'd happened. I sat on the stairs and listened to Dad talking to the police. There'd been an accident, Mark had nearly drowned, and had been airlifted to hospital. He was still unconscious and in a bad way.

Dad hung up the phone and walked slowly into the kitchen, focused on keeping Mum calm. I ran back upstairs, grabbed my coat and threw a pair of boots over my jogging pants. We drove for an hour to Lancaster Hospital in silence. What was there to talk about? We didn't have any information, which feels worse than bad news. I can deal with certainties, even bad certainties, whereas the unknown is a juggernaut of terrifying possibilities. It's the waiting that drives a person mad.

I remember the scene that awaited us in almost photographic detail. Mark's friends huddled together in the waiting area, trying to explain to us what'd happened; Mark on a stretcher, out cold and caked in mud, hooked up to various machines. Now and then he'd regain consciousness and attempt to sit up, thrashing about when they laid him back down. Despite the horrific scene, I was resolutely calm and acted methodically. Mum jumped out of her skin every time that a machine made a beep; I can only presume that she was imagining the 'flat-line' sound that occurs after a patient goes into cardiac arrest. (Thanks, *Holby City*.) I kept reassuring her that the machines were simply taking readings and that it was all standard procedure (not that I fucking knew)!

It turns out that my condition comes in handy during spontaneous, dangerous situations. (They have to be spontaneous.) It's as though my amygdala and primitive senses kick in and can finally be of use. During such moments, a rare clarity comes over me. I'm not afraid of what might happen, but instead focus on what needs to be done.

'They could've made him a bit more presentable!' I joked, trying to ease the tension. Mark's T-shirt had been ripped off completely and dried mud and moss stuck to his body.

A male nurse glared at me, obviously offended: 'Well, you should've seen the state of him when they rushed him in here. He was in a VERY bad way.' He placed great emphasis on the 'VERY' and I wanted to kick him in the balls for putting such an image in our heads. *Cheers, mate.*

I held Mum's hand and continued to talk to her through the machines, while browsing Mark's medical chart at the end of the bed. The nurse wasn't exactly OK with this, but fuck it, I'd already taken photos. I didn't understand a large portion of the medical terminology, nor was I able to decipher the near illegible writing on the paper, but I did understand 'aspiration bacterial pneumonia'. OK, so Mark had water on the lungs that they needed to drain and then they'd pump him full of antibiotics to kill off any bacteria.

I'm not sure how long we all waited by his bedside. Occasionally, I'd try to initiate conversation, but it didn't work. All of us were settled in our personal realms of hell.

A nurse confirmed the diagnosis that we already knew to Mum and me an hour or so later, in a waiting area. 'It's pneumonia, his lungs will need to be drained.'

'Will he be OK?' I asked.

She didn't say a word, which made Mum add, 'He's a young lad, he'll recover just fine, won't he?'

Again, the nurse wouldn't confirm this. Instead, she stood and said, 'We'll do everything we can.'

Is that a liability thing? Are medical staff not permitted to make predictions in any area just in case?

Once Mark was comfy on a ward and we were confident of his treatment, it was time for me to head home. I didn't want to, but the nurses were adamant: only Mum and Dad were allowed to stay, and they promised to ring if there were any updates.

Back at home with no direct outlet for my worries, every irrational fear that was held at bay by seeing for myself that Mark was out of danger bubbled to the surface. *Why couldn't the nurse just tell us that he was going to be OK? Why? Was there something else they weren't telling us?*

Most people would've got on with their evening, had a drink maybe or done some housework to distract themselves. After such a traumatic experience, the brain needs a break. However, pre-breakdown Claire didn't understand that all of her actions were feeding her amygdala.

I literally sat on the kitchen floor and considered EVERY possibility.

I went to bed eventually, clutching the house phone like a lifeline. I remember that *Jackass the Movie* was playing on the miniature TV in my bedroom and my boyfriend at the time was asleep beside me.

I tried to drift off several times but was awoken by a violent internal jolt. After the third or fourth jolt, I had a sudden and overwhelming feeling that if I fell asleep, Mark would die. *Don't be ridiculous. Where the hell has that thought come from?* I was perplexed. Still, once embedded, the thought wouldn't shift. The idea of waking up to the news that he had died was unbearable. Images of his funeral, Mum's face and life without him flashed in my brain and I experienced the accompanying emotions. I was distraught.

So, I stayed alert. It wasn't an effort. My body was already twitching from the adrenaline. I remained on high alert for the next eight hours. It was a reaction to the lack of control I had over the situation. My brain had decided that I might not be able to help literally, but I could, however, stay awake all night to stop him from dying. (Seriously, what the fuck?)

When the sun rose, I rang Mum. 'Is he OK? Is he all right?' I boomed into the handset.

My mum, sounding groggy and confused, answered, 'Yes, of course, he's fine. I told you I'd ring if there was any news.'

I felt foolish for such an outburst and ended the call quickly.

It would've been better in the long run to just admit: 'I'm terrified that he's going to die!' and release all the fear and trauma from my mind. Yet, somehow, saying it out loud felt selfish and a little too intense for a 6 a.m. chat! At the time I had no idea that I was developing an anxiety disorder.

Mark made a full recovery and was back home within a week. I never did tell him about my bizarre night-time vigil.

When I moved to London, that particular beast of a symptom, the one that associated sleep with danger, stayed behind, but when I returned to live in the house all those years later, it emerged from the depths with a force. As though dormant for years, just waiting. Things rarely go away forever just because we want them to.

It started off small initially. I'd wake up with a jerk in the middle of the night, sweating and confused. *Why have I woken up? What's wrong?* I put it down to a nightmare that I had no memory of. Then over the months, the severity of the systems slowly got worse. Along with sweating, my heart pounded so hard it was painful, and my vision was blurred. Then there was the screaming, I'd wake up shrieking without knowing why. I mean like proper, blood-curdling screaming. Which would prompt Dan to yell, 'What, what? Fucking what!'

Eventually I had to acknowledge that something was up. The subconscious, kept at bay during waking hours, had free rein during the night and it was projecting all the shit that I'd been repressing. Not the on-the-surface, anxiety shit, but the deep, dark demons that I'd long buried.

Something important (and obvious to everyone but me) to know about stress and anxiety: you cannot suppress it forever. It will eventually surface in areas that you can't control, sleep being a major one. The brain will find a way to communicate an internal problem.

During this time, I also went through a period of lucid dreaming, which is when you know you're dreaming and are able to control what happens – that was a laugh. Most of the time I'd try and wake myself up shouting or running head first into a wall. 'This is ridiculous!' I shouted at an old lady wearing a headscarf who had materialised in my parents' dream-world house. 'I'm asleep, we all know it. Can you please do something seeing as I've somehow projected you into my subconscious?' She ignored me and continued smoking a cigarette, so I stormed out of the living room.

The worst of all, however, were the night terrors. I still experience them occasionally when I have a bad cold, or I'm stressed. If you've never had a night terror, I'm glad. Save yourself the horror and don't google them. (Basically, you're semi-awake, but unable to move, and you see some really disturbing shit.) Most people report an evil entity being present, or a demon that sits on their chest, slowly suffocating them. I see a hooded figure either at the foot of the bed or standing directly over me. (The hood is ludicrous and frankly very over the top for a bedroom audience.) On one occasion, he grabbed my left ankle and pulled it towards him. Another time he slapped my shoulder, but the worst incident by far was when he grabbed a handful of my hair and yanked it back. Half-conscious I can do nothing except remind myself that, 'It's OK, I'm asleep, this isn't real' and attempt to wriggle my toes and fingers to wake myself up.

I rarely mention the night terrors to anyone because it tends to make people uncomfortable. 'Oh gosh, Claire, I don't know how you cope,' they say, horrified. I tell them not to worry about it and move on.

How do I cope? I don't know. How does one cope with anything? We just do. It's not like he can actually harm me.

Eventually things got so bad that my brain began to associate the very idea of sleep with danger, and as the fog of slumber began to take hold my amygdala triggered a jolt that shot through me like electricity. *NO!* it hissed. *Stay awake!* I'd then momentarily, in my confusion, forget how to breathe, which triggered a bout of hysteria and a full-blown panic attack. 'You can't breathe when you're asleep, you'll forget, and you'll die!' It was an incredibly difficult period, not to mention exhausting. Unlike daytime panic symptoms, the night panic was disruptive to others as well as me. I spent many nights on the couch, concerned about keeping Dan awake.

Like food and water, sleep is essential. How the fuck was I going to get myself out of this one?

When they say that the best way to fall asleep is to 'not think about it', they're technically right. However, this is of no use whatsoever to a person who experiences night-time panic attacks. If anything, it's a cruel taunt. If I told you not to think about giant pink elephants, where does your brain immediately go? Exactly.

I dealt with this new symptom in two ways. First of all, I went to see an EMDR (eye movement desensitisation and reprocessing) shrink, possibly the best shrink I've ever seen. Predominantly used in trauma, the charity PTSD UK explains the treatment: 'The human mind uses REM [rapid eye movement] during sleep time to help it process daily emotional experiences and when trauma is extreme, this process breaks down and REM sleep doesn't bring the usual relief from distress. The EMDR process is thought to produce an advanced stage of the REM processing. As the brain, via the eye movement, processes troubling images and feelings, resolution of the issue can be achieved by dampening the power of emotionally charged memories.'[3]

In a nutshell, EMDR digs out subconscious trauma that has become buried and helps the patient to reprocess painful memories in a healthy way. Anne, my therapist, instructs me to think of my brain like a database and it's her job to help me go through my 'search history'.

Considering that I began most therapy sessions feeling embarrassed and rambling about how 'this isn't going to work on me, because this type of shit never does', I surprised myself every time, to put it politely, by singing like a canary a mere fifteen minutes later. This was normally followed by a storm of rage or tears. On one occasion, my subconscious started speaking through me. *Why do you hurt me so much? I'm trying to help you, but you hate me. Please stop, we're a team. I love you.*

I knocked over a glass of water, screamed and jumped up with a start. It was too much. Fortunately, Anne managed to calm me down. I couldn't believe that I'd had such a powerful reaction to this therapy and at such speed! Especially seeing how I can't meditate, and mindfulness makes me angry. Something about EMDR just clicked and my subconscious used it to communicate.

After this session, I had the same dream every night for a week. Weird. I dreamt of a large black dog, part Great Dane, part Rottweiler, that I knew was called Tallulah, Tally for short. Every night. She sat next to me outside as I sat on a hill. We didn't interact, I felt safe and calm.

Anne referred to the dog as being my 'spirit animal'. This is an old tradition valued by indigenous people. A spirit animal is an aid which helps guide or protect a person throughout life's journey and whose characteristics that person embodies. While the notion was foreign to me, I did appreciate the sentiment. A part of me did wonder if Tally embodied my subconscious. I still call her Tally when I'm talking to myself; it's easier to deal with if I think of my subconscious as a separate entity.

The second trick I deployed was the old accept-and-wait one. I'd get out of bed to disrupt the vibe, walk to the bathroom and run cold water on my hands. (A change in temperature can be used as a gentle shock to the nervous system.) Then I'd look at myself in the mirror and say the following: 'You know what this is. It's a panic attack, no different to any of the others. You're not dying and you're not going to suffocate. It's a trick. You're safe.'

Then I'd go back to bed, lie on my back and let the sensations wash over me. I didn't count sheep, play a memory game or try to think about something else. I'd lie with panic and let it have its moment. Like with all the others, the acceptance did the trick.

Nine out of ten times, panic just wants to be heard, then it'll let you rest.

CHAPTER 13

Yes, You Fucking Can! Breaking Through Barriers

*W**ell, yet again we find ourselves in another shitshow of your making. Congratulations. Look at all the other people around you, they're professionals and you're just a fake. You'll break, and you know it. You can't possibly get through this. Stop now before something really bad happens . . .*

I'm staggering up a hill with – no joke or exaggeration – a 70 per cent gradient. The only thing to hold on to is the barbed-wire fence to my left and I'm very aware that if I trip now, I'll be falling backwards for a long time, taking out other participants as I go, like a bowling ball. I'm freaking out, except that for a change, the reasons for my panic are clear: I'm trekking up a fucking mountain and my legs are about to give way! I can taste blood, my lungs are burning and the sound of my heart, thundering in my chest, is drowning out the podcast I'm listening to. So, I take to chanting 'fuck, fuck, fuck' with each step.

Months earlier, I was approached by a PR company who asked whether I wanted to take part in a half-marathon in the Cotswolds for charity, and I thought, 'Why not?' A spontaneous decision indeed, one of many that I've regretted immediately afterwards, like the time I decided to cut all my hair off or try Bikram yoga.

Except this time, I wasn't the only one affected by my actions. I dragged one of my best mates with me. When the PR rep said I could bring a friend along to run with me and stay in the fancy hotel the night before, I was sold. I knew exactly who to invite, my darling namesake Claire. Claire is one of those beautiful and bizarre people who runs for pleasure. She does park runs on a Saturday morning, when I'm still in my pyjamas, contemplating a shower.

We hadn't spent much quality time together in a while and I stupidly thought the whole experience would be like a mini holiday. So, I said yes, enticed by the 'free stuff' (because I'm shameless) and 'for a good cause' angle (because this balances out the shame).

Alas, they neglected to mention the Bear Grylls endurance shit, or the mud. This wasn't your standard half-marathon, it was a trek that included hills, climbing and uneven terrain. I'm glad that I was green to all this beforehand and even more so that I didn't bother to research the route. Blind ignorance was kinder.

Here's the thing. I'm not a runner. I know that a lot of people say this with a playful laugh and a roll of their eyes, but I'm deadly serious. This especially applies to outdoor running or jogging, as they say. I don't like it, and I'm shit at it. I can run, of course, if the occasion calls for it. If I was being chased by an axe murderer, for example, or I spotted a tenner on the floor. But actual regulated jogging is something that I've just never clicked with.

Maybe it's because I'm a sprinter. As a teenager I even competed on behalf of my school. If I'm honest I only did so for the popularity boost, because the experience was largely unpleasant. The noise, the pressure, the anger, the threat of failure, Mrs Leigh screaming at us all to 'get it done!' You'd think it was the bloody Olympics, not Lever-hulme sports day! Still, I needed something positive to mark me out at that point, so sprinting it was! Waiting on the start line I'd feel sick, my legs turning to jelly, and my heart pounding so hard I could see it through my T-shirt. (Sound familiar?) Yet when that gun fired and the race began, all my energy was channelled into launching myself forward. Everything went quiet as I harnessed the power of all that extra adrenaline. It was magical almost, my mind and body being united.

I behaved exactly how panic wanted me to and was galvanised by it.

I have a chip on my shoulder (which could aptly be labelled a prejudice), about the type of people who jog (Claire and a few others excluded). Maybe I've been exposed to the wrong people, but the ones I have met engage in what I like to call 'sugar judgement'. Sugar judgement is being really sweet about another person's run initially, but then being quick to point out how much further they ran that morning ... with two broken legs and a hernia!

'Oh, a 5K, wow, that's amazing, bless you! My son Roman just did his first ever race today too. He's eight. I can't believe how quickly he finished.' (A whole ten minutes before I did.) *Fuck you, Roman!*

Running, like a lot of natural activities, has become slowly com-mercialised. It starts with 'Couch to 5K' and ends with global marathons that require either a lottery win or charity representation to enter. Seriously? Can't we just go for a run without the admin? By 'we' I mean 'you'. I'll wait in the pub.

The guy who ran the first marathon fucking DIED by the way: 'The first marathon commemorated the run of the soldier Pheidip-pides from a battlefield near the town of Marathon, Greece, to

Athens in 490 BC. According to legend, Pheidippides ran approximately twenty-five miles to announce the defeat of the Persians to some anxious Athenians. Then keeled over and died.'[1]

And people call me mad.

At the Mind awards one year, I found myself talking to a bloke who had run 365 marathons in 365 days and my first response was 'Why?', followed by, 'I've had over three hundred panic attacks.'

He looked confused. 'Is that similar?'

'Well, both activities make us want to shit ourselves!'

Sprinting was easy, it came naturally for me and was over in less than a minute. Jogging, on the other hand, is a skill, as I was about to learn. A skill that requires dedication and patience.

'If you're serious, then you really should have a "Prime Performance armband" for your phone,' the bloke in Decathlon tells me, as I'm shopping for new jogging attire.

'Why? I'll just stuff it down my bra like I always do.'

I once went swimming with a pair of knickers in my hair (I'd run out of bobbles). Am I proud of this? No. But they were black knickers, so I like to think they went unnoticed.

Still, resolved to make positive changes, I take his advice and invest in some new gear. I don't want to embarrass myself or Claire more than necessary.

Picture this scene the following day ...

Kitted out in the new fancy sports gear, I leave the house, ready to go for my first pre-planned training jog. I have an audiobook poised to play, a water bottle in hand and a baseball cap in case the sun decides to make an appearance/I need to hide. I start to jog.

10 seconds in – *Am I running correctly? I feel like I'm running weird.*

15 seconds in – *Those women are staring. Great. I must look like a dick.*

20 seconds in – *I don't like this, I don't like it, I feel stupid.*

25 seconds in – *I can't catch my breath, I can't breathe. My heart is beating too fast, I'm going to keel over. Something's wrong. It's been thirty seconds, I am literally the most pathetic person on the planet. I can't do this.*

45 seconds in – *STOP, NOW!*

90 seconds in – *Oh fuck this, let's go home.*

The only app to ever successfully make me run for more than two minutes without intrusive thoughts was Zombie Run. Turns out I will run very fucking fast if I think I'm being chased by a flesh-hungry member of the undead. Unfortunately, I got a little 'too' into the narrative and started screaming out loud as I ran.

The reality of what I'd agreed to and *who* I'd agreed to do it with began to sink in two weeks before the race. Claire had a six-month-old baby at the time, who was delivered by C-section, which therefore prevented her from training properly. Still, even with this extra challenge, I knew that she would still run circles around me. We're opposites, Claire and I. Think a calm, organised and composed version of me, with blond hair and a strong moral compass. She's the anchor and I'm the ship surging towards the rocks screaming, 'I'm sure we'll be fine!' By this analogy, I'm not exactly sure what I bring to the friendship, besides, trouble and the F word.

I once completed a 5K run at 8 a.m., hungover and in the freezing January cold, for this woman. It was one of her requested hen do activities and I was happy to oblige. I did it partly because I love her, yes, but also because she'd been banging on about 'park runs' for ages, the art of them and all that, and I very much took the attitude of: 'I'm proper fast, I bet I can beat you at this, without training at all.' (Because I'm a dick with foolish notions.) Barely sixty seconds in and I knew I'd made a huge mistake. My friend Jane was next to me and we shared an 'oh bollocks' look multiple times. Claire finished a good fifteen minutes before I did and was only mildly out of breath. I, on the other hand, pretended to be fine, was sick in a bin, and then went back to the hotel for a lie-down on the bathroom floor.

So not only was I going to fail the half-marathon, but I was going to fail in front of a semi-professional who made it look easy-breezy. *Great*.

The big race

My brain doesn't respond well to discomfort, I knew that. It somehow equates it with danger, rather than something that can be managed. Unfortunately for me, running is discomfort embodied. So how I found myself in rural countryside, sweating like a pig and using my arse muscles to power me up a hill, is beyond me.

On the morning of the race, Claire turned into a machine. She knew exactly how many calories we needed to consume, how much water, what our route was, how often we should urinate, where the pit stops would be and how to correctly strap up your feet. She darted across the hotel lobby, making sure we were registered and getting our T-shirts. I stumbled after her like a lost child. My cocky, 'oh I think all runners are knobs' attitude had well and truly evaporated and even though I'd been training for three *cough* two and a half months, I was scared. I looked at Claire helplessly. 'I'm going to slow you down, I know I am.'

'It's not about times, it's about finishing the race. We'll do it at our own pace, there's no pressure.'

Our ideas about pace differed somewhat. The bitch was like a jockey with a whip!

I had my first attack at the start line, but fortunately we'd be running in a moment, the very thing my amygdala wanted me to do!

OMG, OMG, we're running, this is it ... like this is actually it.

Then we were off and I got caught up in the initial excitement. Everybody looked so happy and positive. People had even come out of their homes to cheer us on.

I checked my Fitbit every few minutes, which is both a blessing and a curse for those who experience panic attacks. A blessing because it tracks your heart rate, proving that it hasn't exploded, but a curse because it highlights a spike or rapid increase in your pulse. All of us take our heart for granted and barely pay it any attention at all until something 'feels off'. Incidentally, have you ever failed to find your heartbeat? That's a fun few minutes. *Seriously, I can't find anything. Am I dead? Am I actually dead?* The alternative being heart palpitations. A drumming that feels erratic and out of control.

Ninety minutes in, at the top of that hill, I was amazed by what I saw on my Fitbit screen. The highest I'd ever recorded during a panic attack back home was 141 bpm. It was 2 a.m. and I was sprawled out on the floor in the kitchen, helplessly watching the numbers increase with each beat. According to the NHS guidelines, 188 bpm was my absolute max. Any higher and I was in heart-damage territory. I had 999 already keyed into my mobile and my thumb hovered over the call button. Yet, as the minutes passed, and I used my standard calming techniques, the number reduced, and I had no need for emergency services. Can we take a second and imagine THAT conversation?

Emergency operator: 999 Emergencies, what is your emergency?
Me: MY FITBIT SAYS I'M ABOUT TO DIE!

Well, at the top of that mountain (fucking huge hill), in that moment, my heart's bpm reads 174. Higher than *any* panic attack has ever taken it. 'I can't do this!' I scream at Claire, no longer caring about embarrassing myself. My lungs are on fire and my thighs are shaking from the exertion, my heartbeat deafening in my ears. 'Claire, I'm not fucking joking, I can't do this!'

Used to my explosive nature, she simply responds, 'Not too much further.'

Incredulously, I glare at the back of her head and I surge forward, waiting for my chest to explode. I can't last much longer, I know it. *You don't have a choice. What are you going to do, ring a taxi? Just focus on putting one foot in front of the other. Keep moving.*

'I can see the top!' Claire yells.

I don't believe her but continue to move.

With one final push, we break over the tip of the hill and on to level ground. I'm seeing stars and a light grey mist forms across my eyes as I bend over, gasping for air. I look down at my Fitbit, which now reads 177 bpm. 'Oh my god, my heart!' I gasp, horrified. 'I can't catch my breath! It's so tight, I can't breathe!' I feel the panic crash over me like a tidal wave. *You're going to keel over right here.*

I look desperately at Claire, who opens her backpack and retrieves a chocolate brownie (good pit stop snack). 'That was hard, I'm out of breath too,' she says breezily.

I'm incredulous again, why isn't she more concerned? 'No, seriously, this isn't right!' I snap.

She hands me the water. 'My heart is beating fast too, that was quite the workout, you should be really proud! Let's take a few minutes to rest and then carry on.'

I want to shake her I'm so livid. 'Listen to me, I think something is wrong!' I'm like a child in the final stages of a tantrum. She barely acknowledges it and again responds breezily and confidently, 'You're fine!'

I look down at my Fitbit: 173 bpm. The people around us are breathing hard and sweating too. Some are sitting on the ground and one man is actually being sick.

A quick side note on heart attacks by the way, as panic attacks are frequently confused with them (not surprising if your heart is pounding like a drum). I wrote a very popular post on the key differences, which you may find comforting.

Differences between a heart attack and a panic attack

(Disclaimer. I am NOT a doctor. The below is based on research and lived experience.)

- Panic attacks produce more 'body-wide' symptoms than a heart attack, for example, you feel like a thousand things are happening at once: heart palpitations, difficulty breathing, but also, sweating, dry mouth, heavy limbs, nausea, stomach cramps.

- The pain during a heart attack is constant and more constricted. It starts in the chest, stomach or lower back areas and can sometimes move down the left arm. Whereas 'tingles' are more associated with panic and can spread to every limb.
- A heart attack *doesn't* strictly affect a person's breathing. Hyperventilating is more associated with panic. That's a comfort to me when I have a panic attack at night and wake up gasping for air.
- A panic attack tends to come in waves. It rises and falls. Whereas the symptoms of a heart attack remain constant.
- With heart attacks, the pain normally occurs during movement, whereas for panic, it mainly occurs when resting. Think excessive adrenaline that needs to be released. Hence, why exercise can be helpful.

Breathing heavily and dripping with sweat, it suddenly hits me like a sledgehammer to the gut: *this is normal.* How did that never occur to me? *This reaction you're having right now is normal.* Of course, my heart is pounding, I've just trekked up a sodding mountain! Could it be that my body was stronger than I thought? That it wasn't weak and pathetic after all? I was having a Bryony Gordon moment. In her book *Eat, Drink, Run* she writes about the moment running saved her: 'Sweat poured into every crease and wrinkle of my flabby skin. But I felt alive again.'

Trust your body

I realised that panic had a knack for convincing me to throw in the towel. *This is too much. I can't stand it. Stop now before something awful happens.* It was 'self-protection' taken to extremes.

I'd learned from the 'rule of opposites' that my instincts weren't always accurate. So, as much I wanted to give up and find some first-aiders, I did as Claire asked. I drank my water, we rested for two minutes and then continued.

Nothing happened. Time passed and I didn't die.

'I didn't die, I was just really uncomfortable!' I shouted behind her, completely stunned by such a simple, but explosive realisation.

She smiled. 'That's running. So much of it is in the mind. I didn't say anything because you were panicking, but I struggled on that hill too.'

This was the correct course of action. Any indication that she was less than 100 per cent calm would have sent me into a frenzy. (In any relationship only one of you can freak out at once, you have to take it in turns. That's the rule.)

I'm a very all-or-nothing person. I'm either great or shit, there's no in-between, and I'd been applying this 'perfectionism' mentality to running. I'd been saying to myself that if I couldn't do it without stopping, or without experiencing discomfort, then I should just give up. What's that saying? *If at first you don't succeed, then get the fuck out.* (Not actually a saying, but works for me.)

As Claire and I continued, I thought about running as a skill. *There's nothing wrong with me, I'm normal. This was normal.* As sports journalist Monica Olivas writes: 'There's always a learning curve when you start a new hobby, or sport. Just because running doesn't involve a ball or a bat, doesn't mean that you don't have to learn how to run. Most of the time our mind quits before our body does. It requires training and practice.'[2] Panic had previously tricked me into quitting at the first signs of discomfort.

After believing that my body was weak for almost a decade thanks to both panic and anxiety, I was stunned by this new-found appreciation. The adrenaline that I'd been afraid of for so many years, had enabled me to reach the top. My heart had reached a bpm higher than any panic attack had ever taken it and I was not only still standing, I also felt fine. Psychologist Trevor Powell refers to the 'loss of control' that panic can cause. Anyone can lose faith in their own abilities because of 'misinterpretations of what is actually going on'. My adrenaline had been deployed to assist me rather than to hurt me.

I spoke to self-proclaimed reluctant jogger Mike Richards, an IT executive from Manchester.

I run to remind myself of how strong my body is. Panic attacks made me believe that my body was fragile, as though I might have a stroke or collapse at any moment. Running gave me a sense of power and reminds me that everything is working exactly as it should. A pounding heart is not a sign that I'm about to have a heart attack, but a natural reaction to physical exertion. It beats faster to provide the necessary blood flow to the muscles.

There were several other moments during the half-marathon where I couldn't catch my breath or worried that my bpm was too high, but

I took comfort in a new-found confidence. My body wouldn't give up on me. It was stronger than I realised.

I can't write that after the half-marathon I discovered a love of running, because I didn't. I still find it tedious. But I have a new respect for the activity and those who do it. Jogging, I realised, can teach a person endurance, discipline and motivation. For many, it's a great way to maintain their mental health. This is a category that I also find myself in these days. I might not love exercise, but I recognise the positive impact it has on my brain. I run to keep my head straight.

What I discovered during this experience was an appreciation for my body and, despite how fragile panic can make me feel, my bulk is a shield against the world, an anchor. I won't snap like wheat in the wind, or a fragile bloom. My body will claw and foam and trudge its way to safety whether I'm having a panic attack or not. As a control freak, it was hard to accept that any part of me could function without conscious thought, knowing its job automatically. My amygdala was wrong, my body could and would operate safely without the need for constant supervision.

The half-marathon taught me how to harness the power of a panic attack, using the rush of adrenaline, rather than feeling enslaved by it. When Claire and I crossed the finish line, hand in hand, I felt more empowered than I ever have in my life. I had faith in myself and felt that maybe, just maybe, everything would be all right after all. Which is a pretty big deal for a cynic.

The End Bit

As I write this now, I'm sitting in my gym gear about to go for a run ... am I FUCK!

I'm waiting for the Uber Eats delivery guy to bring my McDonald's breakfast. (I might have an addiction to Egg McMuffins and hash browns. Seriously, I've taken the wrappers to public bins before now, because Dan noticed how often I was having them. One time I even paid cash to bypass the paper trail!)

I'm not great with conclusions, I never was at university (because I couldn't wait to finish my dissertation) and I'm going to struggle now because I don't have one great nugget of wisdom to share. My story isn't over. I still live with panic and I'm OK with that.

When Nadiya Hussain asked me if I thought I'd ever be fully cured, I didn't know how to answer, because I'm not sure I really need curing. I don't see panic attacks as being an illness in a traditional sense, more of a symptom.

Sarah Wilson believes that we experience anxiety when we're not connected with our true selves, and I'm inclined to feel the same about panic. 'By going down to the dark depths, we finally made the

235

connection. Because anxiety, eventually, inevitably, makes us sit in our shit. It takes us there, to the darkness. It forces us to do the journey. And only then can we see what we're looking for. We can see the truth. We see it all as it is.'[1]

It takes guts to sit with fear and I mean really sit with it, alone, not knowing if you'll ever come out the other side. To let it crash over you like a wave without resistance, when every fibre of your being is telling you to rebel. Mental strength doesn't come into the equation, after all we're all the same in the dark. The natural reaction is to fight, to push the unpleasantness away and desperately try to think happy thoughts. Sometimes I wonder if we just haven't been taught to process negative emotions in the way we process happy ones. It took me a long time and hundreds of panic attacks to understand that when all the noise and rage subsides, panic is really trying to do one thing ... communicate.

I think I've always known that the attacks weren't random. That they weren't some evil entity seeking to derail my life. I just struggled to decode the messages they carried. Sort of like a twist in a horror film, when the protagonist realises the ghosts haunting them were actually trying to warn of greater danger. Also, I'd spent the better part of a decade sedating every negative thought in my head with alcohol and prescription medication. So, it's not surprising that nothing coherent came through.

What was the message? There's been a few, but the main one took root finally when I caught sight of my reflection in the toilets, on that dreaded night in A&E. I saw it in my eyes as my jaw spasmed painfully. I was void, gone and completely empty. For the first time in my life, I had nothing left to give. No fight or strength. To put it bluntly, I was killing myself. Slowly, but there was no doubt I was fading.

If I carried on treating myself this way then I would die young, either from natural causes or suicide. I'd already considered jumping in front of traffic that night and I don't like to think what could have happened if Dan hadn't shown up when he did. He knew it too – I saw it in his eyes. Fear, for me.

Self-love is the last lesson I learned and it proved to be the hardest one to implement. I refused to take care of myself, so panic forced my hand for the final time that night, by essentially incapacitating me. Extreme, but necessary.

That's been the pattern all along. My subconscious continually tries to inform me that I'm unhappy, lost and hurting myself, and I refuse to listen, blindly ploughing ahead. The panic attacks were the trump card, the one thing that always made me stop and listen, even if I didn't understand the message.

I could hardly be expected to understand *what the fuck are you doing? You're miserable! Let's reassess your life later at home* when I was on the bus struggling to breathe and sweating like a drug mule! I was focusing on the physical symptoms triggered by the fight-or-flight response.

Self-compassion doesn't come naturally, it isn't an ingrained quality that we're all born with. It's a skill that needs to be practised regularly, and I needed a lot of practice! Writing things down helped initially; no joke, I used to make a checklist of basic self-care: Food? Water? Sleep? Fresh air? Downtime? Interaction with family and friends? I had to implement it as a new habit, rather than trying to change old ones. Whenever I felt the urge to punish myself, I think of that girl in the mirror, staring back at me, bruised and broken.

I stopped giving so much of myself away professionally and now wait a minimum of twenty-four hours before committing to a project (even the ones that I'm excited about). Again, this was a structured habit that I had to practise.

Even without all the heavy emotional stuff, panic has taught me so much. To ask for help when I needed it, to be mindful about nutrition and to allow myself to make mistakes without reprimand. I couldn't have evolved without either of my breakdowns and, as horrific as they were, living miserably forever would have been worse.

I wish I had all of the answers (and not just because I'd be super-famous). Not all of the attacks could be attributed to something concrete. Sometimes, I just had a panic attack because I was tired, or hungover, or scared of flying. My amygdala was sensitive, like a smoke alarm running low on batteries.

I mentioned at the beginning of this book that the key to panic attack management is 'time' and I still believe this to be true. When an attack is particularly bad, I look at a clock for comfort and remind myself that nothing can defeat the progress of the hands moving steadily clockwise.

Believe me when I say that you can learn to manage panic attacks, just as you would an allergy. It's a pain in the arse, but necessary and not so bad once you plan ahead.

Three hundred plus attacks down and I'm still standing. Panic might knock me on my arse, but I get up, I ALWAYS get up.

Helpful resources

NHS 111
Helpline: 111 (Talk to a call handler 24/7 about symptoms)

The Samaritans (Volunteers are available to chat via phone 24/7 365
    days a year)
Helpline: 116123
Website: https://www.samaritans.org/

No Panic
Crisis number: 01952 680835 (Recording of the breathing technique
    played 24/7)
Helpline: 0844 967 4848 (Available from 10 a.m. to 10 p.m. every
    day of the year)
Website: https://nopanic.org.uk/about-us/

SANE
Helpline: 0300 304 7000 (Available 4.30 p.m. to 10.30 p.m. every
    day of the year)
Website: http://www.sane.org.uk

Check Point (A website that identifies local websites and emergency
    contact numbers on an international level)
Website: https://checkpointorg.com/global/

Endnotes

Chapter 2: What Does a Panic Attack Feel Like?

1 https://www.scientificamerican.com/article/what-happens-in-the-brain-when-we-experience/
2 https://www.thescienceofpsychotherapy.com/the-triune-brain/
3 https://www.medicalbag.com/home/features/despicable-doctors/walter-freeman-the-father-of-the-lobotomy/
4 David Carbonell, *The Panic Attacks Workbook*, Ulysses Press, 2004
5 Sarah Wilson, *First, We Make the Beast Beautiful*, p. 62, Corgi, 2019

Chapter 3: The Big Trick: Why Panic Attacks Happen

1 https://hbr.org/2018/09/curiosity
2 https://medium.com/@tylertervooren/why-833ec0ed1ddb
3 https://www.livescience.com/9125-woman-fear-intrigues-scientists.html
4 https://www.nationalgeographic.com/science/phenomena/2010/12/16/meet-the-woman-without-fear/
5 https://www.theguardian.com/commentisfree/2019/jan/14/obsessed-success-early-in-life-sally-rooney-youth
6 David Carbonell, *The Panic Attacks Workbook*, p. 47, Ulysses Press, 2004
7 Susan Cain, *Quiet: The Power of Introverts in a World That Can't Stop Talking*, p. 31, Penguin, 2013
8 Mrs Moneypenny, *Mrs Moneypenny's Careers Advice for Ambitious Women*, p. 49, Penguin, 2013

9   *How to Fail with Elizabeth Day*, 'S2, Ep1 How to Fail: Jessie Burton', 3 October 2018, https://howtofail.podbean.com/e/how-to-fail-jessie-burton/
10 Elizabeth Gilbert, *Big Magic*, p. 110, Bloomsbury, 2015
11 https://www.dazeddigital.com/beauty/soul/article/44463/1/commodification-self-care-good-thing
12 Emma Gannon, *The Multi-Hyphen Method*, Hodder & Stoughton, 2018

Chapter 4: Panic on Stage: Public Speaking and Dealing with Your Inner Voice

1   Robert Graves, *Goodbye to All That*, p. 144, Penguin, 2000 (new edition)
2   https://www.ncbi.nlm.nih.gov/pubmed/7754283
3   Roger Baker, *Understanding Panic Attacks and Overcoming Fear*, Lion Books, 2011
4   https://www.anxietycoach.com/claire-weekes.html

Chapter 5: Panic at Work and Laughter, the Superpower

1   https://www.adzooma.com/blog/mental-health-crisis/
2   https://www.thescienceofpsychotherapy.com/the-triune-brain/
3   https://www.theguardian.com/commentisfree/2020/apr/29/coronavirus-lockdown-anxiety-mental-health
4   Emma Gannon, *The Multi-Hyphen Method*, Hodder & Stoughton, 2018
5   Barbara Crăciun, 'Humor as a defense mechanism and working instrument of the cognitive-behavioural therapy', *Romanian Journal of Cognitive Behavioral Therapy and Hypnosis*, vol. 1:1, 2014, https://pdfs.semanticscholar.org/7404/dfb72073808da32e29571cd8f2564b512fce.pdf
6   https://adaa.org/learn-from-us/from-the-experts/blog-posts/consumer/anxiety-find-humor-find-cure
7   Brian King, 'Health-Related Benefits of Humor and Laughter', seminar sponsored by the Institute for Brain Potential, Los Banos, California, 2018, https://www.ibpceu.com/content/pdf/LGH-DL-outline.pdf

Chapter 7: Who's Flying this Plane? Airports and Travel

1   https://www.stratosjets.com/blog/fear-of-flying-statistics-trends-facts/

2 https://www.huffingtonpost.co.uk/entry/why-does-flying-make-us-so-emotional_uk_5dea673de4b0913e6f8f070f?guccounter=1&guce_ref errer=aHR0cHM6Ly93d3cuZ29vZ2xlLmNvLnVrLw&guce_referrer_sig=AQAAACZ6qqrlXEkwxVfU1OdVQ5dPyKMHAuhcD2ZJaRv4H Uiwxam5N8NbihuNKcgnqI6VOH6uO1Yaj7paQ9S3kzN8Hldiq EIj0vh3eRNE-vTl6sRxGLRLI8dcFqNSmWiV_rHmaLMGb6_0Y9GRguundXRmsApamr_YovMYbnyYgu2Q-kTR
3 https://www.neverendingfootsteps.com/how-i-overcame-my-fear-of-flying
4 https://www.anxietycoach.com/breathingexercise.html
5 https://www.youtube.com/watch?v=2hGGHcjMMa4
6 https://www.nzherald.co.nz/travel/news/article.cfm?c_id=7&objectid=12145193
7 https://internewscast.com/naomi-campbell-poses-in-a-hazmat-suit-with-goggles-a-surgical-mask-and-rubber-gloves/
8 https://www.youtube.com/watch?v=wQ0LjVp0fvs
9 Derren Brown, *Happy*, Corgi, 2017
10 David Carbonell, *The Panic Attacks Workbook*, p. 161, Ulysses Press, 2004

Chapter 8: Act Normal: Dating, Relationships and the Relationship You Have With Yourself

1 https://www.glamour.com/gallery/50-dating-dos-and-donts
2 Shahroo Izadi, *The Kindness Method*, Bluebird, 2018

Chapter 9: Learning to Talk About Panic

1 https://www.heysigmund.com/vulnerability-the-key-to-close-relationships/
2 https://www.mindful.org/why-is-it-so-hard-to-be-vulnerable/

Chapter 10: Help! Educating Those Closest to Us

1 https://www.sciencedaily.com/releases/2016/10/161005102031.htm
2 https://www.psychologytoday.com/gb/blog/evolution-the-self/201706/feeling-understood-even-more-important-feeling-loved

Chapter 11: Gut Instinct: Looking After Your Brain with Food

1   https://www.health.harvard.edu/diseases-and-conditions/the-gut-brain-connection
2   https://www.sciencedaily.com/releases/2019/09/190906092809.htm
3   https://www.symprove.com/chloe-brotheridge-anxiety-and-the-gut/
4   https://www.alcohol.org/alcoholism/#alcoholism-definition--what-is-alcoholism-or-alcohol-use-disorder-
5   https://www.healthline.com/nutrition/caffeine-withdrawal-symptoms#section4

Chapter 12: Night Panic

1   https://www.bbc.com/future/article/20120522-suffer-from-sleep-shudders
2   https://www.businessinsider.com/what-is-a-hypnic-jerk-2014-5?r=US&IR=T
3   https://www.ptsduk.org/treatment-options/eye-movement-desensitisation-reprocessing-emdr/?gclid=CjwKCAjwh472BRAGEiwAvHVfGsIuG4LcbKlc8HSm3D33ctv4M4CdizdRmb0h5cBZ6vLJdLtYscRCHRoCrygQAvD_BwE

Chapter 13: Yes, You Fucking Can! Breaking Through Barriers

1   https://www.livescience.com/11011-marathons-26-2-miles-long.html
2   https://www.active.com/running/articles/7-common-running-fears-and-how-to-conquer-them

The End Bit

1   Sarah Wilson, *First, We Make the Beast Beautiful*, p. 299, Corgi, 2019

Acknowledgements

First of all, this book wouldn't have been possible without my legend of a husband Dan, and my dog Rigby. Thank you both for your endless patience, love and encouragement. You are my heart.

To my family and closest friends, gratitude for the love, yes, but also for sharing your lives in these pages, which I have exploited!

Thank you to the following people for your mental health expertise: Natasha Devon, Ruth Cooper-Dickson, Aaron Gillies, Ellen Jones, Rachel Winterbottom, Louise Gates, Lotte Mikkelsen, Dr Soph and Gabriel Nathan. You make me sound smarter by association and I'm lucky enough to call you mates.

Thank you to my agent Richard, who reins in my trigger-happy nature and keeps me on track. Thank you to Rowan Yapp, Mireille Harper and Clare Sayer at Square Peg. I'm chuffed to be part of the imprint.

A huge thank you to Justine Taylor for helping me develop the book and for dealing with my frequent emotional outbursts! You played an invaluable role.

Finally, thank you to everyone who reached out in September 2019, both online and in person, when I experienced a mental breakdown. Especially, my anonymous Twitter friend 'Just me and Fellini', and Lorraine the paramedic for showing kindness I will never forget.